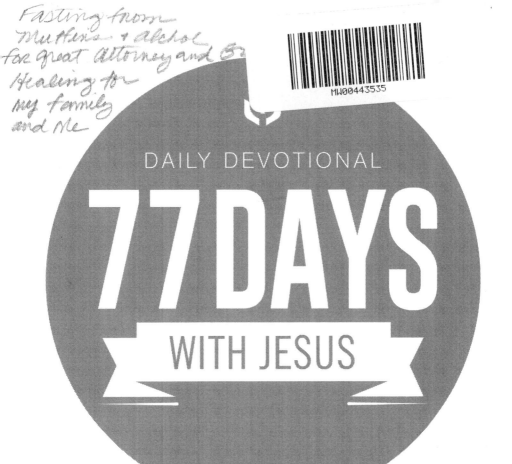

Fasting from Mutters + alcohol for great attorney and healing to my family and me

DAILY DEVOTIONAL

77 DAYS

WITH JESUS

God, Please open my mind and my eyes so that I may learn all that I need to Glorify you — so that I may know you better and hear when you speak to me. Give me wisdom and help me retain all that I need to be closer to you.

KNOW HIS LOVE AND HEAR HIS VOICE

PASTOR CHUCK BOOHER

ISBN-13:
978-1539879558

ISBN-10:
1539879550

Jesus Said That The Key To Eternal Life Is That We "Know" Him.

He desires to have a real relationship with you, where you know His love and hear His voice. For far too many people, Christianity has been nothing more than a "religion". However, God, our Father, intended for us to have a true connection with Him; by knowing Jesus, God is revealed to us in a very powerful way.

This journal will guide you, in 77 days, to know Jesus; *really* get to know Him. You will know who He is and what He values. You'll understand how He acts and reacts. You'll see what He loves and how He shows love to you and others.

When you know Him this way then you will experience life, as He intended, for the very first time! Jesus called this the "abundant life." It is so incredible that it cannot be imagined, seen or described to others; it can only be experienced. This new life can only be known when you have a relationship with Him as your Savior, Lord and Friend.

So, I am praying you will come to really know Jesus over the next 77 days. I am hoping you fall in love with Him, as I have. I pray that you connect with Him, and by doing so, you hear His voice, know His presence and experience His promises.

WHAT DO THESE VERSES SAY TO YOU?

John 17:3 (NASB)
> 3 *"This is eternal life, that **they may know You**, the only true God, and Jesus Christ whom You have sent.*

John 10:14-16 (NASB)
> 14 *"I am the good shepherd, and **I know My own** and **My own know Me**, 15 even as the Father knows Me and I know the Father; and I lay down My life for the sheep. 16 "I have other sheep, which are not of this fold; I must bring them also, and **they will hear My voice**; and they will become one flock with one shepherd.*

1 John 5:20 (NASB)
> 20 *And we know that the Son of God has come, and has given us understanding **so that we may know Him** who is true; and we are in Him who is true, in His Son Jesus Christ. This is the true God and eternal life.*

Jeremiah 9:23-24 (NASB)
> 23 *Thus says the LORD, "Let not a wise man boast of his wisdom, and let not the mighty man boast of his might, let not a rich man boast of his riches; 24 but let him who boasts boast of this, **that he understands and knows Me**, that I am the LORD who exercises lovingkindness, justice and righteousness on earth; for I delight in these things," declares the LORD.*

Jeremiah 31:33-34 (NASB)
> 33 *"But this is the covenant which I will make with the house of Israel after those days," declares the LORD, "I will put My law within them and on their heart I will write it; and I will be their God, and they shall be My people. 34 "They will not teach again, each man his neighbor and each man his brother, saying, 'Know the LORD,' **for they will all know Me**, from the least of them to the greatest of them," declares the LORD, "for I will forgive their iniquity, and their sin I will remember no more."*

Hosea 6:3 (NASB)
> 3 *"So let us know, **let us press on to know the LORD**. His going forth is as certain as the dawn; And He will come to us like the rain, like the spring rain watering the earth."*

THE CHRONOLOGY OF THE MINISTRY OF CHRIST

While there is a general agreement among Bible Scholars concerning the order in which events took place in the ministry of Christ, some of the details of those events vary. In most cases, the discrepancies are minor. Understand that each of the Gospel writers had a different perspective and purpose based on the audiences they were addressing.

I have spent hours studying, praying and seeking to know the true chronology of these events. In this journal, we journey with Jesus from His baptism to the Cross in the order I have been shown.

HOW TO GET THE MOST OUT OF THIS JOURNAL

My goal for this journal, is to stimulate your quality time with the Lord, as we seek Him and desire to learn from Him. Use the following techniques to ensure you get the most out of this journal.

- Use a Bible version most compatible with this journal: NASB, ESV, HCSB, New King James

- Set a time each day to be with the Lord. Be intentional about this and make it a priority.

- As you begin your quality time with Him, pray. Ask Him to teach you and guide you as you progress through the journal.

- Read each passage and really pay attention to what Jesus says and who He is. Seek to understand what is happening. Think about who Jesus is interacting with and how He communicates with them.
- Write down your insights as they come. Write down any questions you have.

- Close your time by writing a prayer, sharing with Him what you have learned and what you feel you've been called to do with it.

WHO IS JESUS?

Jesus is God.

- God took on flesh to live among us. He impacted the world more than anyone before him or to come. Why?

- To bring you close to God, so that your sins could be forgiven and you would be cleansed completely.

- So that God would become your Father.

- So that you would know Him.

Jesus did all of these things in an area smaller than the state of New Jersey with no modern communication, and yet the world has never been the same. James Francis said this so well in his poem, *One Solitary Life*.

He was born in an obscure village
The child of a peasant woman
He grew up in another obscure village
Where he worked in a carpenter shop
Until he was thirty when public opinion turned against him
He never wrote a book
He never held an office
He never went to college
He never visited a big city
He never travelled more than two hundred miles
From the place where he was born
He did none of the things
Usually associated with greatness
He had no credentials but himself

He was only thirty-three

His friends ran away
One of them denied him
He was turned over to his enemies
And went through the mockery of a trial
He was nailed to a cross between two thieves
While dying, his executioners gambled for his clothing
The only property he had on earth

When he was dead
He was laid in a borrowed grave
Through the pity of a friend

Nineteen centuries have come and gone
And today Jesus is the central figure of the human race
And the leader of mankind's progress
All the armies that have ever marched
All the navies that have ever sailed
All the parliaments that have ever sat
All the kings that ever reigned put together
Have not affected the life of mankind on earth
As powerfully as that one solitary life

LIFE GROUP LEADER GUIDE

As you go through this journal, you'll read daily passages that will help connect you to the heart of Jesus, hear a message about applying those scriptures to your everyday life, and discuss it in fellowship with others during your LIFE Group.

We've included questions at the end of each week so your LIFE Group can discuss what you're learning as you journey through 77 Days with Jesus.

When you gather with your group, consider using this format to get the most out of your time together:

- Connect with one another (10-15 min)
- Pray for your time together (1-3 min)
- Discuss the questions together (30-35 min)
- Practice what you've learned this week (15-20 min)
- Close by asking how you can be praying for one another (5-15 min)

2/26/17
3/5/17

DAY 1

Jesus is amazing because He was, and is, both completely God and man at the same time! There is no way that we can completely grasp the miracle of who He is, and yet He revealed Himself to us in an incredible way.

Read John 1:1-18, and as you do, think about how significant it is that John begins our introduction to Jesus in this passage.

Write down the truths you are told about Jesus in John 1:1-5. *The word was God and the word is with God. All things were made thru him and without him nothing was made. In him was life and the life was the light of men.*

And the light (God) shines in the darkness and the darkness did not comprehend it.

What are we told about John the Baptist's mission in verses 6-7?

John was sent by God to be a witness and bear witness of the light — that all through him might believe

Look carefully at verses 9-13. What does this tell you about how people reacted to Jesus? What does Jesus promise to those who receive Him?

He was the world - and the world was made thru him - and the world did not know him. He came to his own - and his own did not receive him. Jesus was the true light which gives light to every man coming into the world. But to those who received him — to them he gave the right to become children of God — To those who believe in his name who were born not of blood, nor the will of the flesh, nor the will of man, but of God.

8

Read verses 14-18 in the New American or English Standard Version. Write down what this tells you about Jesus and how we are to be in relationship with Him.

Jesus is among us and we beheld his Glory - The Glory as the only Begotten of the father - full of Grace and truth. This is he - he who comes after me is preferred before me - for he was before me - and of his fullness we have all received - and Grace for Grace. For the law was given thru Moses but Grace & Truth came thru Jesus Christ.

Read Colossians 1:15-20.

Write down each of the attributes it reveals about who Jesus is.

Jesus is the image of the invisible God - The 1st born over all creation. For by him all things were created that are in heaven & earth - Visible & invisable wheather thones or dominations or principalities or powers. All things were created through him and for him - and he is before all things and in him all things consist. He is the head of the Body - the Church who is the beginning, the first born from the dead that in all things he may have the preeminence. All the fullness should dwell in him & by him to reconcile all things to himself by him

Read Philippians 2:5-16.

What does this tell you about Jesus? Write down every specific aspect you learn about who He is. Jesus was made in the likeness of man. He was humble and obedient to the point of death. God gave Jesus the name which is above all names. Jesus Christ is Lord to the Glory of God the Father

What do these verses call us to do so that we will be truly His? Why is this important? How does the way we speak and live impact Jesus?

That the name of Jesus every knee should bow of those in heaven and those on earth & those under the earth. And that every tongue should confess that Jesus Christ is Lord - to the Glory of God the Father - Do all things with out complaining & disputing

Of what you read today, what stands out to you most?

That those who receive Jesus he gives the right to become his children and that Jesus Christ is Lord

Write a prayer asking Jesus to reveal Himself to you. Ask Him to mold you into His image so that you will be more like Him.

Father God - I pray that you reveal yourself to me. Please mold me into your image - so that I will be more like you.

Father give me wisdom to understand and comprehend when I am studying this Journal and Bible.

Father I want you to know that I love you and seek to follow your word and make you proud.

In Jesus name I pray

Amen

DAY 2

Jesus chose to begin His public ministry in a desolate setting. The Judean desert is dry, hot and ugly. John the Baptist used the Jordan River to baptize those who would come to him, and come to him they did.

John's baptism location was either the very place where Joshua led the Children of Israel into the promised-land by miraculously crossing the Jordan River or it was very close to that spot.

Here, Jesus would enter the waters to be baptized and begin to change the world.

Where: Days 2-4 of this journal take place in the Judean Desert near the Jordan River.

Read Matthew 3:1-17.
What was John's message and purpose, according to verses 1-3?

*Repent for the Kingdom of heaven is at hand
For this is He who has spoken of by the
prophet Isaiah*

*Prepare the way of th Lord
Make his paths straight.*

Look at verses 4-6. What was John like and how would that have made him more effective?

*John was clothed and his food was wild locust
and honey, Then Jerusalem, Judes and
Jordan region went out to John and
were baptized by him in the Jordan River
and confessed their sins*

Look at verses 8-10 again. What was John's message to the Pharisees? What does he tell them to do? What does he warn them not to trust in? What is the warning John gives in verse 10?

What lesson can you learn from this?

Look at Luke 3:11-14. Write down what John tells the crowds, tax collectors and soldiers to do.

What would John have told you to do to bring forth the fruit of repentance?

Look back at Matthew 3:11-12. What does John tell us about Jesus?

What do we learn about Jesus in Matthew 3:13-17?

Why was Jesus' baptism necessary to His public ministry and effective leadership?

Write a prayer asking God to reveal how you are to bring the fruit of repentance. Ask God to show you if there is something you need to do to fulfill all righteousness in your life.

DAY 3
Jesus: His Ministry Begins

Jesus began His public ministry with fasting and prayer. Think about that. He had been waiting 30 years to grab hold of His destiny and He begins by spending focused time with God the Father. He will fast and pray for 40 days then He will enter into temptation.

Read Matthew 4:1-11.

Look at Matthew 4:1-2 along with Luke 4:1-2. Write down how the Spirit was moving in Jesus. What does this tell you about what it means to be Spirit-led? Why was fasting and prayer essential to the beginning of Jesus' ministry?

What does this tell you about the importance of your fasting and prayer? What do you think would happen if you chose to fast from something for 40 days?

Read Matthew 4:3-4. What is the first temptation the Devil uses against Jesus? How does Jesus defeat this temptation?

What does it mean that we live on every word that proceeds from the mouth of God? What is a practical way to do this every day?

Look at the second temptation the Devil uses against Jesus in Matthew 4:5 There was a belief among the Jewish people of Jesus' day that the Messiah would appear by floating down from heaven in front of the Temple. Knowing this, what was Satan tempting Jesus to do?

How did Jesus respond to this temptation and what was He committed to in His life?

Now we come to the next temptation found in Matthew 4:8-10. Also, read Luke 4:5-8. From what you read in Luke, why did Satan say he can offer Jesus all the Kingdoms of the World? What does this tell you about why there is so much evil in the world?

What did Satan tempt Jesus to do and what did he offer Him?

How did Jesus respond? Can you say that was true of Jesus? Would you say that is true of you?

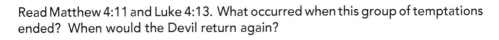

Read Matthew 4:11 and Luke 4:13. What occurred when this group of temptations ended? When would the Devil return again?

What are some things you learned from Jesus that you can apply to your own life?

Write a prayer asking the Holy Spirit to fill you and lead you to become someone who lives by every word that proceeds from the mouth of God, serving God and Him only. Ask Him if there is an area of your life where you need to change so that you are living according to God's Word. Ask Him to reveal how you can commit to serving Him.

DAY 4
Jesus: His Ministry Begins

Jesus is still in the Judean wilderness, in close proximity to John the Baptist, where he was baptizing people. As Jesus walked by John's location, two of John's disciples saw Him.

Read John 1:35-51.

Look at verses 35-39. What did John say about Jesus? What does that tell you about Him? John sent two of his disciples to follow Jesus. What does this tell you about John?

Jesus' habit as a leader was to lead with questions. When Jesus asked, "What do you seek (or want)," He is asking something profound. How would you answer Jesus? What do you want from Jesus? Take your time to think about this. What do you want Him to do for you and/or with you?

John is able to recall the time of day this specific moment happened. Most likely it was 4 PM. John wrote this nearly 60 years later and he still remembered the exact moment and time.   Have you ever had something happen that was so incredible that you remember the exact day and time it occurred? What does this tell you about the impact Jesus had on John? Has Jesus ever had a similar impact on you?

Now read John 1:40-42.
What did Andrew do now that He has met Jesus? What did he say about Jesus?

What did Jesus say about Peter? Why is the name change so significant? What would Jesus say about you?

Now read verses 43 to 51 again.
What did Jesus say to Philip? What would this mean to him?

What did Philip tell Nathaniel? What was Nathaniel's response?

When Jesus met Nathaniel, He told him something that no one could have possibly known. How did this effect Nathaniel? What did Jesus promise him?

Take some time to really think about what you have just seen and learned about Jesus. Write a prayer answering the questions, "What do you want?" and "What do you seek?" Ask Jesus to reveal what He wants for you and from you.   Ask Jesus to guide you as you follow Him.

DAY 5

Jesus is now traveling from the Judean wilderness to the beautiful area of Galilee.

Jesus has been invited to a wedding in Cana. He brought his first followers with Him and in the midst of the wedding feast He will give them the first sign that He is the Messiah.

The wedding and the feast that followed was a joyous time of celebration and they wanted to be able to experience this event with the whole community. An essential part of the celebration was wine.

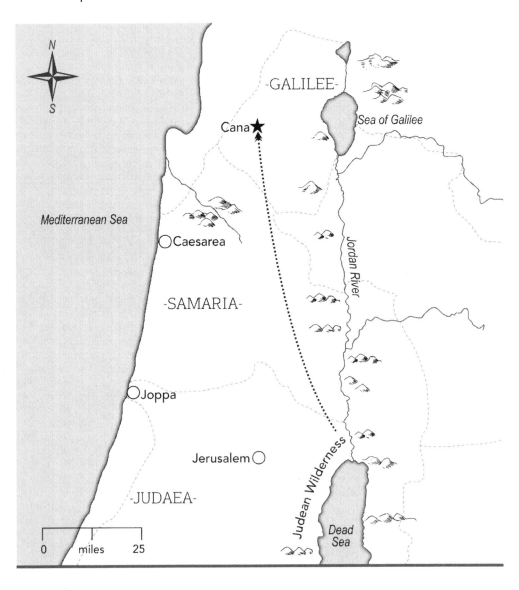

Read John 2:1-11 and pay close attention to verse 11.
Look back at verse 1-5. What did Mary ask Jesus to do and why did she ask Him to do it?

A key to this miracle taking place was the faith statement of Mary; "Whatever He says to you, do it." Why did this lead to a miracle? What would have happened if the servants refused? What is your reaction to that statement in regards to your life? What will happen if you do all He tells you to do?

Focus on verses 6-10. How much faith would it take to give the water to the headwaiter?

Jesus turned the ordinary into the extraordinary. What does this tell you about Him? What should this mean to you in your relationship to Him?

What lesson can we learn about the fact Jesus not only turned water into wine, but turned it into the best wine?

Read Romans 8:28. How does this promise relate to what Jesus did for the couple getting married?

Read verse 11 and write down what this first great sign is telling you about Jesus. What does this tell you about how He felt about Mary? What does this tell you about what He wanted His disciples to see and then know?

Write a prayer asking Jesus to show you what He wants you to do. Ask Him to take ordinary things in your life and make them extraordinary. Ask Him to take the moments in your life that are not good (like running out of wine at a wedding feast) and turn them into good because you love Him and will do all He tells you to do.

DAY 6

One of the most important feasts God instituted was Passover. In this feast, the Jewish people were to remember that God "passed over" their sins as he visited judgment on the Egyptians. God did this because they had the blood of a lamb on their doorposts. This pointed to a day when God would give His only Son as a sacrifice for us so that He would "pass over" any judgment that should come upon us.

While Jesus would have celebrated Passover every year, this year He used the power of the Spirit to show the people of Jerusalem that He was the Messiah God had promised.

Jesus traveled over 90 miles from Galilee to Jerusalem.

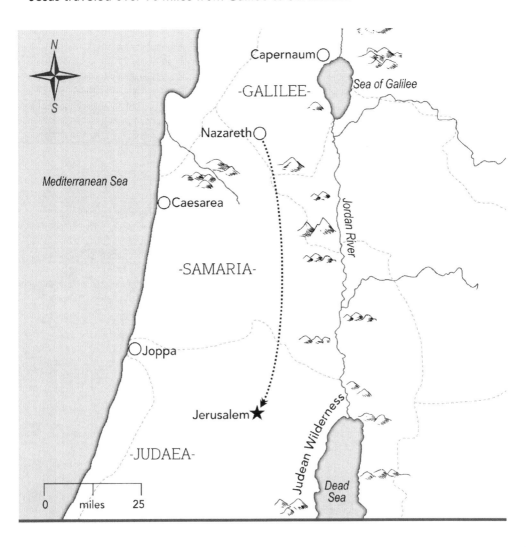

Read John 2:12-25
When Jesus came to the Temple area he found merchants who are ripping off the people. Animal sacrifices and monetary offerings had to be ceremonially cleaned. The merchants would sell the animals and exchange money at a premium, extorting the people as they came to worship God.

Look at verses 13-16. What did Jesus do when He entered the Temple area? Why did He do it? What is the significance of overturning the tables with doves on them?

Jesus did this with a whip and no one stopped him. What does this tell you about Jesus' physical strength and stature?

According to verses 17-18, what are the reactions of His disciples and the religious leaders?

Look at verses 19-22. What was Jesus' response to them and what did He mean?

John 2:23-24 tells us about Jesus' insight regarding what people are really like. What does this tell you?

What did you learn about Jesus today? What stands out to you and why?

Write a prayer asking Jesus to cleanse any area of your life that is not pleasing to Him.

DAY 7
Jesus Travels to Jerusalem

Jesus is still in Jerusalem for the Passover. He receives a visitor in the night, and not just any visitor, but one of the most prominent men of the Jewish nation. Nicodemus was a respected Pharisee, who were very pious and religious people. He was also a member of the Sanhedrin, an elite group of 70 men who ruled the Jewish people and land under the Romans. Outwardly, he was popular, successful and respected, yet even he needed a Savior. From this encounter, it appears he knew it.

As you read John 3, notice how much Jesus loves this man.

Looking at verses 1-2, what was Nicodemus' view of Jesus? What is the significance that Nicodemus, an older and far more educated man, calls Jesus, "Rabbi"?

As you read verse 3, write down exactly what Jesus says must happen for anyone to see and be a part of the Kingdom of God.

Now focus on verses 4-8. What is the difference between being born in the flesh and born in the Spirit?

How does the fact we can hear the wind and see the effects of the wind without actually seeing the wind relate to the way the Holy Spirit works?

Read verses 9-15. What does Jesus tell us about Himself? What does He say we must do to receive eternal life?

Now study verses 16-18.
What does God do and why? What does God want us to do so that we will not perish but have eternal life?

How does John 3:17-18 give verse 16 a clearer and deeper meaning?

Looking at verses 19-21, why is it that some come into judgment?

If we are going to practice the truth then what must we be willing to do?

In verses 22-36, what do we learn about John and what do we learn about Jesus?

God so loves you that He wants to give you love and life. Write a prayer and share honestly about your belief in Jesus. If you do believe in Him, explain why and what it means. Tell Him you want His love and that you want to live in the light. Share your willingness to be transparent about who you are and how you live.

▪LIFE GROUP DISCUSSION QUESTIONS▪

DISCUSS THESE QUESTIONS TOGETHER:

1. What is one thing you learned about Christ from Day 1 in the journal?

2. In Day 2 of the journal, Pastor Chuck prompted us to see why Jesus' baptism was necessary to His ministry and His effective leadership. How did you answer the question? Why is it important for you to do the same?

3. Matthew 4:3-4 shows us the first temptation Satan uses against Jesus and how He overcame it. What do you see Satan commonly using as a temptation in your life? How do you defeat such temptations?

4. In Day 4 of the journal, Pastor Chuck guided us through John 1:35-51. Specific reference was made to verse 39 in which John recalls the exact hour he followed Jesus to spend the day with Him. In this passage, John is recalling this moment with Jesus 60 years after it took place! What personal experiences can you recall with such detail?

5. In Day 7, we learned the difference between being born in the flesh and born in the Spirit. What is the difference we find in John 3:4-8?

■LIFE GROUP DISCUSSION QUESTIONS ■

LOVE LIKE JESUS

Read John 3:19-21, Matthew 5:16 and 1 John 2:9-10. What does this tell us about Christ's love for us and the way we are called to love others? What effect does "walking in the light" have on others and how is that an outward sign of an upward love?

INTENTIONAL INTIMACY

It is said that we cannot see wind but can hear and see the effects of it. How have you seen and heard the effects of the Holy Spirit this week?

FULLY SURRENDERED

Read John 2:1-11. What lesson is to be learned by Jesus turning water into the wine? What "water" are you hesitant to bring before Him? Why are you not surrendering it to Him? Dream and imagine with your group what God could turn that into.

EXPERIENCE MORE

Read Matthew 28:19. How can you experience more by living out this verse?

DAY 8

Jesus is preparing to travel from Jerusalem to Galilee knowing He must go through Samaria. There, racial tension was so great that Jews were not safe. Yet, Jesus had to go through Samaria for someone who mattered to Him, when she felt she mattered to no one.

Jesus arrived at noon, the warmest time of the day. Because of the intense heat, people would avoid the wells mid-day. Genesis 24:11 tells us the most common time to get water was in the evening when it was cooler. Only a social outcast would go to the well at noon.

Read John 4:1-45.
In verses 7-9, why was the woman surprised that Jesus asks her for a drink? What barriers was Jesus willing to break to reach out to her? What barriers should we be willing to break to reach out to others?

Study verses 10-15. How did Jesus get her attention? How did he pique her curiosity? What did He promise her? What is the thirst you have in your life? What is the only way we can truly have satisfaction?

What would it mean to have a well of living water spring up inside of you?

Now read verses 15-24.
What issue did Jesus bring to light that needed to be dealt with before she couldhave the living water she desires?

Five men had divorced her and the man in her current relationship would not marry her. How would this make her feel? How is this related to the time of day she chose to get water? Why did Jesus mention it?

Why is it significant that Jesus was alone with her at the well? How does this show the way Jesus loves? Who needs you to love them in this way? How can you show it?

How did she react to the way Jesus treated her and talked to her?

Look at verses 23-24 again. What do you learn about God? What does God value?

Who does Jesus tell her He is in verse 26? This is the first time He reveals who He really is. Why now? Why to her?

Looking at verses 28-42, how did this encounter with Jesus change her self-worth and value to her community?

Now go back to verses 30-38. What can we learn from Jesus about how we are to live and what we are to value?

Write a prayer asking Jesus to show you how much you matter. Now ask Him to identify people in your life that need to be shown that they matter. Ask Him to surprise you by placing people who need love and care in your path.

DAY 9

The region of Galilee is where Jesus did the majority of His teaching and miracles. While he was raised in Nazareth, Capernaum became His new home; more specifically, Peter's home became His home. Take some time to review how long Jesus had been openly ministering. Look at where He has been by going over what you have learned so far.

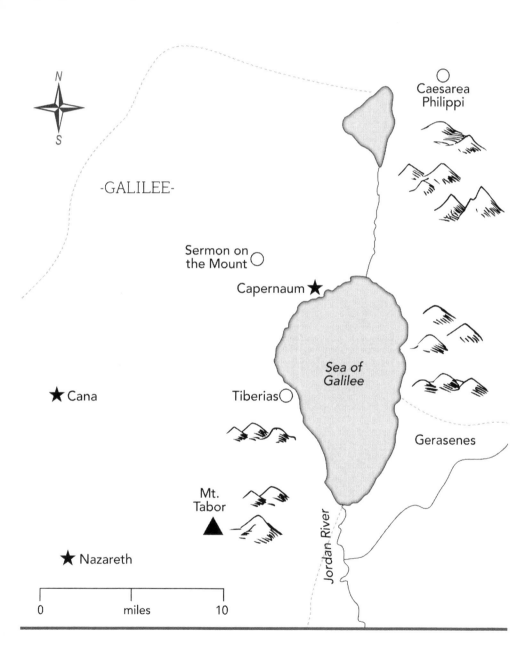

Read Luke 4:14-30.
Looking at verses 14-15, how did Jesus return to Galilee?

What did He do and what was the result?

Look at verses 16-21 again. What was Jesus' custom?

Jesus intentionally went to the scripture Isaiah 61:1-2, the prophecy of the coming Messiah. Note how it starts with the Messiah having the power of the Spirit of God. Compare that to verse 14 in this chapter of Luke. What are the five things Jesus says He is called to do?

What did Jesus promise in verse 21 and what was the reaction of the people?

What did Jesus say in verses 23-28 that angers the people?

Try to picture in your mind what happened in verses 28-30. What does this tell you about the power of Jesus?

Look back at the five aspects of Jesus' ministry as the Messiah. Which one do you need for Him to enact in your life the most? Can think of someone that needs one of those aspects of Jesus' ministry? Write a prayer asking Him to move in your life and in the lives of others.

DAY 10
Jesus Returns To Galilee

Reflect on all that Jesus has done and said up to this point. Think about the time that has passed since His baptism and first meeting of Peter, Andrew, James and John.

Jesus and His disciples are now at the Sea of Galilee (also known as Lake of Gennesaret). Jesus is going to ask these men to take an important step, transforming their lives and changing the world.

Read Luke 5:1-11.
What were Peter, Andrew, James and John doing? Where had they been all night and what was their business?

What did Jesus ask Peter to do in verse 3? Look at Matthew 4:12-17. What message was Jesus sharing?

Now look back at Luke 5:4-7. What did Jesus ask Peter to do and what was Peter's response?

Who would appear to know more about fishing, Peter or Jesus? Who actually knew more? Who knows more about you and your life, you or Jesus?

What was Peter's reaction to the amazing catch of fish Jesus directed them to?

What direction did Jesus now give to Peter and the others? How would that apply to you and your life?

These men left everything to follow Jesus. They would keep their boats and return home to Capernaum, but Jesus had become their priority. Is that true of you? Write a prayer asking Jesus to share His calling for you. Ask Him to show you your purpose. Tell Him you are fully committed to following Him.

DAY 11
Jesus Returns To Galilee

John the Apostle shared seven of Jesus' signs that proved Him to be the Messiah and Son of God. The first was turning water into wine at the Wedding feast in Cana of Galilee. Now that the men have left all they had to follow Him, they are ready to see the second sign. This sign will show that Jesus' power and authority are beyond space and time.

Where: Jesus is in Cana which is approximately 20 miles from Capernaum.

Read John 4:46-54.
How did the father feel in this story?

What did Jesus say about people and what they want?

How did Jesus' words and promise effect the father according to verse 50?

What was the significance of knowing the very hour the son was healed? What does this tell you about Jesus and His power?

The first sign was turning water into wine. The second was healing the royal official's son from over 20 miles away. What do these two signs mean?

Write a prayer telling Jesus that you trust Him and believe in Him. Tell Him you know that nothing is too hard or too far for Him. He can turn any life or situation into a miracle.

DAY 12
Jesus Returns To Galilee

Jesus' ministry was powerful, but also personal. He taught with authority and He showed care. There was a large synagogue in Capernaum that Jesus taught in. A short distance from the synagogue was Peter's house where Jesus would stay.

Read Mark 1:21-28 and Luke 4:31-37.
What was Jesus' teaching like?

How did the demons react to Jesus?

What does this tell you about Jesus' authority?

Read Mark 1:29-31 and Luke 4:38-39.
Why is the healing of Peter's mother-in-law significant? What was her reaction to Jesus healing her? How would this apply to your life?

Read Luke 4:40-44.
What does this tell you about Jesus' power and purpose? How did Jesus handle the desire of the crowd with the calling He was to fulfill? What did Jesus do to reenergize after ministering to the large crowd?

Write a prayer asking Jesus to meet a need in your life, like He did for Peter. Include a prayer of commitment asking Jesus if there is a way you can serve Him now.

DAY 13
Jesus Returns To Galilee

Peter, Andrew, James and John's fishing business was located at the Sea of Galilee. They were seasoned fishermen and they knew the dangers of this great lake. Even now, when storms hit, the wind swirls with such power that large boats with engines can be in trouble. A group of men in a row boat would be no match for a great tempest.

Read Mark 4:35-41. This is Peter's account of what happened.

What did Jesus ask them to do and what was their response?

How bad was the storm that hit them?

Look at verse 38. Where was Jesus and what was He doing? What does this tell you about Him?

What question did they ask Him? Have you ever wondered if the Lord cared about what you are going through?

In verses 39-41, what did Jesus do and what did He ask?

What did they learn about Him?

Do you have faith in Jesus? Do you believe He can handle the storms of your life? Write a prayer asking Him to meet your needs, calm your storms and increase your faith.

DAY 14
Jesus Returns To Galilee

Jesus is now taking His disciples on an adventure to the Gerasenes area (also Gadarenes) which was on the other side of the Sea of Galilee. Here they encountered two men, although one stood out so much that Mark and Luke talk only about him.

Read Mark 5:1-20.
What is the description of this man in verses 1-5?

What happened according to verses 6-10? What does this tell you about Jesus?

A "legion" is six thousand soldiers. Look at Matthew 12:43-45. What does this tell you about what happened to the man? What does this tell you about what could happen to others?

Look at Luke 8:31. Where were the demons afraid of being sent? Read Revelation 9:1-12 which describes what happened to the demons in the abyss during the last days. What does this tell you about the demons? What does this tell you about the state of the demon-possessed man in this passage and why he needed Jesus?

Now looking at Mark 5:11-17. What happened? What was the reaction of the people in the region? Are there people today who know that Jesus makes a difference, yet want nothing to do with Him?

In Mark 5:18-20, what did the demon-possessed man want? What did Jesus tell Him to do?

Write a prayer listing some of the great things the Lord has done for you. Ask God to create opportunities for you to share your stories with others.

■ LIFE GROUP DISCUSSION QUESTIONS ■

DISCUSS THESE QUESTIONS TOGETHER:

1. Read John 4:10-15. What "thirsts" do you have in your life? Where do you attempt to quench those thirsts? Where is the true satisfaction found? What does it mean to have "a well of living water spring up inside of you?"

2. In Luke 4:14-30, Jesus returns to Galilee filled with the Spirit. His return was received differently. How are we received when we go into a situation with the Spirit? How are we received when we go into a situation without the Spirit? Give an example of a time when you did each and share how the outcomes varied.

3. How often do you catch yourself operating in a way that would suggest you know more about a situation or topic than Christ does? Share a personal example of this with your group. Now read Luke 5:1-11. Who knew more about fishing: Jesus or Peter? What can you learn from this story and how can you apply it to your life?

4. Read John 4:46-54. What is the significance of knowing the hour the son was healed? What can we learn about God's timing from that? Does this reassure you that He will come through on His word or cause you to doubt His plan? Why? Have you experienced something like this firsthand?

5. Share a time with your group when you were in the midst of a difficult storm. What did God call you to do while still in the rough waters? Were you surprised by His promptings? Did you obey Him? What was the outcome? Read Mark 4:35-41 to hear Peter's account of a stormy time.

6. Read Mark 5:11-17. Are there people you know who refuse Jesus, even after seeing the difference He can make in their life? Share about a time Jesus has prompted you to do something and you've ignored Him.

▬LIFE GROUP DISCUSSION QUESTIONS◄

APPLY WHAT YOU'VE LEARNED THIS
WEEK BY PUTTING IT INTO PRACTICE:

LOVE LIKE JESUS

Sometimes, loving others might mean saying "no" to things and resisting the desire to please others before God. Read Luke 4:40-44 to see how Jesus resisted the desires of many and how he re-energized after ministering to others. Take time this week to re-energize so you can continue loving God and loving others the way He's called you to.

INTENTIONAL INTIMACY

Look back to Day 9 of the journal and recall the 5 aspects of Jesus' ministry as the Messiah. Which do you need Him to enact in your life most? Spend time this week in prayer asking Him to move in your life the area(s) you have listed.

FULLY SURRENDERED

If you were asked to leave everything: your car, home and career to, follow Jesus, would you? Ask God to show you where you need to surrender to His will and purpose for your life.

EXPERIENCE MORE

What barriers are you willing to break to reach others? Read John 4:1-45 to see some of the barriers Jesus broke to reach the woman at the well. Jesus went out of His way to show love to social outcasts. Identify someone who might be a social outcast, and do something loving for them this week.

DAY 15
Jesus Returns To Galilee

Jesus sailed back across the Sea of Galilee to Capernaum, when he was implored by the people of the Gerasene to leave. He was met by Jairus, the head of the synagogue, who was frantic because his daughter was near death. Jairus was desperate for Jesus to go with him to heal her, however, a huge crowd of people had formed, wanting to be near Jesus so badly they were pressing in on Him. Because of this, walking to the house would be almost impossible.

There was another distressed person in the crowd. A woman who had been hemorrhaging for twelve years, who was weak and anemic. According to Leviticus 15:25-33, she was not to be around anyone because of the danger of spreading her illness. So, for twelve years, she lived in isolation, alone and lonely. For twelve years, she hoped her health would be restored. She is now risking her life by being in the crowd, just for the hope of touching Jesus and being healed.

As you read this, understand that it was wrong for a woman to touch a man in public; A woman to touch a Rabbi was atrocious. Additionally, for a woman with her sickness, touching anyone could mean her death.

Read Mark 5:21-34.
What did Jairus want?

Remember that Mark is sharing Peter's point of view. What did Peter tell us happened to the woman, according to verse 26?

Knowing Luke is a doctor, what does he tell us about the woman and her condition in Luke 8:43-44?

Look again at Mark 5:28-32, along with Luke 8:44-46. Read the details of the account and write down what happened. What did you learn about what the woman's actions and the result of her actions?

Now read Mark 5:33-34. What did Jesus call her? What would that mean to someone who had been in isolation for twelve years? What does this tell you about Jesus?

Now look at Mark 5:35-43. Think about what you just read. What does this tell you about Jesus? What do you learn about the way He cares and meets our needs?

Write a prayer asking Jesus to draw you close to Him. Ask Him to calm any fears you have. Ask Him to make you aware of His presence when life seems hard or hopeless. Ask Him to make you His child.

DAY 16
Jesus Returns To Galilee

What was a day like in the life of Jesus? On the same day Jesus sailed from Gerasene, He healed the hemorrhaging woman and raised Jairus' daughter from the dead. Then, a few blocks from there, two blind men met Him at Peter's house to be healed. This is followed by a demon-possessed man and a conflict with the Pharisees. In the midst of this, Jesus still cared for all of the people around Him.

How would you feel if you had a day like this, a week like this, a life like this?

Read Matthew 9:27-38.
What did Jesus ask the blind men in verses 27-29?

What was Jesus' response based on?

What does this tell you about how Jesus will choose to answer you? Do you believe Jesus can and will help you? Do you believe He can handle anything you are facing?

Look at verses 32-34 again.
What two reactions did people have to what Jesus had done? Why did these groups react different?

Have you seen people react differently to Jesus? Write down what their reactions were. Why do you think they reacted the way they did?

Looking back to verse 29, what will happen to them, based on their reactions?

Read verses 35-38 again. How does Jesus care for people in verse 36?

What does it mean that they were distressed and dispirited? Have you ever felt that way? Do you notice when other people are feeling that way?

What does "the harvest is plentiful and the workers are few" mean?

Take some time to pray for people who need Jesus to rescue them from distress. Pray God will use you to bring the message of Jesus to them. Pray they will become the workers Jesus is seeking.

DAY 17

Jesus Returns To Galilee

The crowds that wanted to see and hear Jesus continued to grow. Each crowd was filled with friends, enemies and the curious. On this day, some were desperate for their friend to meet Christ. They would do anything to make it happen and that passion matters to our Lord.

Read Luke 5:17. What part of the crowd was filling Peter's house? What did Luke tell us about Jesus?

Now read Mark 2:1-13, where we get Peter's perspective on what happened that day and what happened to his house.

In verse 1, Peter called his house Jesus' home. What does that tell you about his relationship with the Lord? Would that be true for you? Does Jesus feel at home with you?

Focus on verses 3-5.
Who are the people mentioned in this passage?

What obstacle did the friends face and what did they do about it?

How do you think Peter felt about the friends tearing into his roof? How did Jesus feel about it?

How do you think the paralytic felt as he was lowered down in front of Jesus and the Pharisees?

When you care that much about your friends and family, how will Jesus feel about you? Look back at yesterday's reading. How does it relate to the need for workers to be a part of the harvest?

What did Jesus do for the paralytic? Whose faith moves Him to do it?

What was the reaction of the Scribes and Pharisees? How did Jesus know that was their reaction? What does that tell you about Jesus?

These friends were creative in how they got their friend to Jesus. Write the names of some people you want to bring to Jesus. What are some creative ways you can get them there? Ask the Lord to give you ideas. Make a written plan for what you are going to do to make them aware of the love Jesus has for them.

DAY 18
Jesus Returns To Galilee

On the same day Jesus angered the Scribes and Pharisees by healing the paralytic, Jesus took it to a whole new level by befriending Matthew, a tax collector.

Tax collectors were an anathema, someone who was detested, during the time of Roman rule. They were considered traders to the Jewish nation by siding with Rome for monetary gain. They also were known for extorting people to line their own pockets.

Matthew was the tax collector in the town of Capernaum. Peter and the others would have known him and most likely despised him. It is interesting that in the gospel of Mark, which would have been from Peter's perspective, Matthew was called by his full name. Then in Matthew's account, there was something in Jesus' words that really stood out to him.

Read Mark 2:13-22 and Luke 5:27-39.
Focus on Luke 5:27-29. What did Jesus ask Matthew to do? What did Matthew do?

This call would have cost Matthew an excessive amount of money and forced him to give up his job. Do you think you would have done what Matthew did? Do you think most people would?

How did the Pharisees react to Jesus being at this reception with these people? Look at Matthew 11:19. What does it mean that Jesus is the friend of sinners? Should the Church be a place where sinners are welcome?

How did Jesus respond to the Pharisees?

Of the three accounts, only Matthew included what Jesus said in Matthew 9:13. Why was this significant? Why would this be something Matthew would never forget? What does this mean about how we should see and care for others?

Read Luke 5:33-39. What did Jesus us tell us about the old religious ways and the new spiritual ways? What did Jesus say happens when someone is exposed to the old wine of religion in verse 39? Are you a new wine or an old wine person?

Write a prayer asking God to identify people who are far from Him that need your friendship. Pray for ways you can show them love and care. Pray that they will come to Church with you.

DAY 19

Jesus traveled back to Jerusalem for one of the Jewish feasts with His disciples. This was Matthew's first time experiencing Jerusalem with Jesus. On the way to the temple was the Pools of Bethesda. Here, Jesus performed the third of seven signs that John the Apostle called out to show that Jesus is the Messiah.

Read John 5:1-17
Look at verses 1-6. How long had the man been sick and how did Jesus know about his condition?

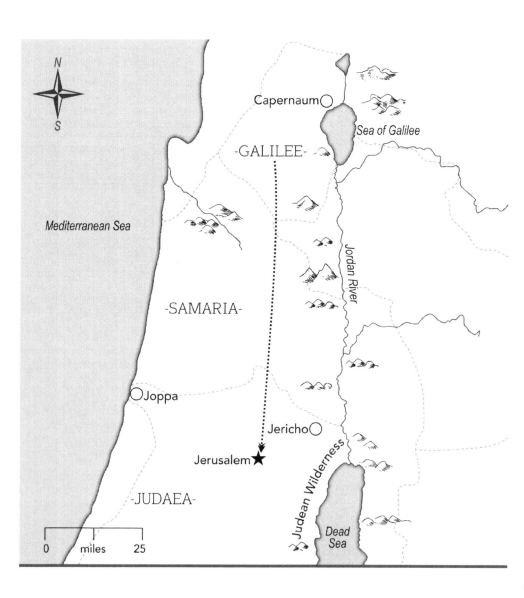

What question did Jesus ask him? Why would He ask this question? Do you know anyone who does not want to be healed or see their condition changed?

In verse 7, what reason did the man give for not being helped? How did Jesus shine a light on the man's real condition?

What did Jesus tell the man to do in verses 7-8 and what the result? Have you noticed how often Jesus wants people to take some responsibility for their own healing? How would that apply to anything that you are facing or dealing with? How does that apply to other people you know?

What does this teach you about Jesus? What does this teach you about faith?

Why do you think Jesus did this miracle on the Sabbath when He knew it would anger the Pharisees? What can we learn from this?

Look at verse 14. What did Jesus say to him? What is Jesus saying about sin? Are there any sins in your life that the Lord is telling you to stop committing?

Why do you think the Pharisees and Scribes were more concerned with religious rules than the miraculous healing of a man who had been sick for 38 years?

What did Jesus' response mean? What does this say about how the Father is working?

Write a prayer asking the Lord to change any situation or condition you are dealing with. What is it that you want changed? What do you want to see take place? Ask Him to reveal any steps He wants you to take before He will intercede for you. Pray for those you know who need to take steps toward healing. Pray they will have the faith to trust that God will work for them.

DAY 20
Jesus Returns To Jerusalum

Jesus, still in Jerusalem for the feast, is now in an increasingly hostile conflict with the Jewish religious leaders. He healed a man who was very sick and hurting for 38 years, but they are more concerned with their religious rules than God's miraculous power. Jesus is unrelenting in taking a stand against them. In doing so, He set a course that will lead to His crucifixion, yet He does not back down.

Read John 5:16-47.
According to verse 18, what two reasons did the Jews have for wanting to kill Jesus?

Read through verses 19-22 and write down what it says about the Father and Son. What are we told about anyone who will not honor the Son? As you read this, what stands out to you the most and why?

What promise is found in verse 24? What must we do to obtain that promise?

Now look at verses 25-29. What does Jesus tell us about the resurrection of the dead and the judgment that follows?

What does verse 30 teach you about Jesus and how He judges?

The Jewish law had a policy which said that for something to be proven true, there must be two witnesses. According to verses 31-38, who gave clear testimony that Jesus is true and to be believed?

According to verses 37-38, why do some hear God and others do not?

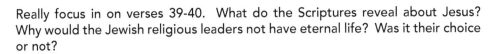

Really focus in on verses 39-40. What do the Scriptures reveal about Jesus? Why would the Jewish religious leaders not have eternal life? Was it their choice or not?

Jesus is telling the religious leaders that the Old Testament points them to Him. There are hundreds of prophecies that foretold of the coming of the Messiah and Jesus fulfilled them all right in front of them. They knew the scriptures, they were just unwilling to believe in Jesus. Why do you think that was the case? Do you know people who are like this today?

Write a prayer asking God to strengthen your faith. Ask him to make you someone who hears His voice and sees Him working. Ask Him to make the scriptures come alive to you. Pray for others you know that need to know Him.

DAY 21

Jesus' continual conflict with the religious leaders is escalating. Leaving Jerusalem and traveling back to Galilee meant a change in venue, but not in legalistic climate. So, as He brings the fresh breeze of the Holy Spirit, it also rubs the religious leaders in an irritating way.

To get the context of what Jesus is dealing with, read Luke 5:36 through 6:5. What does Jesus say will happen if we try to mix the new with the old?

In Luke 5:39, Jesus tells us that when we drink from the old wine we do not want the new. Why does He say this is? Can you see that happening in our churches today? Have you experienced it? If so, what happened?

Look at Luke 6:1-5. In their day, it was permissible to take and eat some grain for energy as you passed by a field. It was not permitted to do so on the Sabbath, because it was considered work. What happened when the disciples did this anyway? Most likely, they never would have done such a thing before meeting Jesus. Describe the effect Jesus is having on them.

How did Jesus answer the Pharisees? Read Matthew 12:3-6. What matters more to God? Do you see the similarity in how He answered them and how He answered Satan? Why would this be important to keep in mind?

When Jesus said that He is Lord of the Sabbath, what did He mean? What does that tell us about His love for the Sabbath? What does that tell us about His authority when it comes to the Sabbath?

Look at Mark 2:27. How does this apply to what Jesus is teaching?

Write a prayer thanking Jesus for setting us free from legalism. Thank Him for allowing us to operate in love and know that compassion matters more than sacrifice. Ask Him to bring to mind people who need your compassion.

◼ LIFE GROUP DISCUSSION QUESTIONS ◼

DISCUSS THESE QUESTIONS TOGETHER:

1. The world shouts many things at us, often times giving us false names or labels. Read Mark 5:33-34. What did Jesus call the woman? What do you think this name meant to her after being in isolation for twelve years? What does Jesus call you? How does he meet us in our times of isolation or loneliness?

2. Read Mark 2:1-13. In this section of scripture we see a few friends do what it means to "jump through hoops" for their buddy. They didn't stop to check how far they were from the nearest Home Depot or Lowes, or even take the time to price out how much the repair of the roof was going to cost. The cost and work were insignificant to the priceless healing their friend was soon to receive. What hoop could you jump through this week for someone you know?

3. Read Luke 5:30-31. When have you caught yourself having the attitude of the Pharisees? How can you shift your attitude and take such thoughts captive?

4. "Responsibility" is a word we are taught as children and hope to have mastered by adulthood. Jesus calls attention to this topic in John 5:7-8. What has God been asking you to take responsibility for in your own life? Why do you think He wants us to take ownership over such things?

5. In John 5:39-40, Jesus shares a valuable lesson. What is it? If you were to witness such things before your own eyes, would you be oblivious or in denial? Have you ever looked back on a time when you turned a blind eye to things Christ was doing for or around you? What caused you to give credit where credit was due?

►LIFE GROUP DISCUSSION QUESTIONS◄

APPLY WHAT YOU'VE LEARNED THIS
WEEK BY PUTTING IT INTO PRACTICE:

LOVE LIKE JESUS

In Day 16 of the journal, we discover Jesus' busy schedule. From healings to casting out demons, He was always being called on in one way or another. After a crazy day, week or even year, He continued to love on those who came to Him. Look past the crazy day you've had and choose to love someone by meeting their need this week, even when you feel "drained."

INTENTIONAL INTIMACY

Often times we get caught up in checking off the "quiet time" box. When we rush through our time with God daily, at weekly services, or in community, we miss the purpose He intended for them in our lives. Read Mark 2:27 to be reminded of why God calls us to spend time with Him and His Church.

FULLY SURRENDERED

Matthew 9:37-38 tells us that "the harvest is plentiful but the workers are few." What does that mean? How can the surrender of your time, talent or treasure help to change that ratio?

EXPERIENCE MORE

Are you surrounded by people who don't know Jesus? If not, how could you experience more by searching out people who need to know about Jesus?

DAY 22
Jesus Returns To Galilee

After the confrontation in the grain field, Jesus goes into the Synagogue. This was His custom on the Sabbath and He would not let them keep Him from it. In the Synagogue was a man with a withered hand. The question is, would Jesus help him or not.

Read Luke 6:5-11. What did Jesus know? What did He do anyway? Why would Jesus not wait a day to perform this miracle?

Look at Matthew 12:9-12. What did Jesus say was so hypocritical about what they were thinking and how they were acting? Do you think that there are people who put the well-being of animals over people? Do you think that is right or wrong?

In Matthew 12:13-14, how did the Pharisees react to this incredible miracle?

Read Matthew 12:15-21. What did you learn about Jesus? Do you see how He reacts differently to people based on their needs? What stands out to you about how Jesus acts and reacts?

Write a prayer telling the Lord what you have learned. Ask Him to open your eyes to those you can help and care for based on what they need in this moment.

DAY 23
Jesus Returns To Galilee

Jesus is well into His ministry now and it comes time to choose the twelve Apostles. Take a moment to think through what has already occurred in the life and ministry of Jesus. What have the Apostles seen and what has He taught them? It is only now they are ready for the calling and position He has for them.

Look at Luke 6:12. What did Jesus do before He appointed the 12 Apostles? Why is this important? How does this apply to any decision you need to make in your life?

Read Matthew 10:1-15. What did Jesus give the Apostles authority over? Was this authority given to only them or to all His followers?

In Matthew 10, verses 2-4, we are given the names of the Apostles. Mark 3:17 tells us James and John were nicknamed the "Sons of Thunder." In Matthew 10:4 we are told that Judas would betray Jesus. Write down the names of each Apostle and what you know about them. What stands out as you look at this list of men who would change the world?

Note how clear Jesus' instructions are to these men. In verses 4-6 who are they told to go to and not go to? Would there come a day they were to go to the Gentiles?

According to verse 7, what message are they to preach?

In verses 8-10, what are they to do?

In verses 11-15, how are they to live?

A good leader gives responsibility, authority and clarity to those who follow him. What do you learn from Jesus about being a great leader?

Write a prayer asking Jesus to clarify what you are called to do and how. Ask Him to show you how to lead others in your life with the same clarity.

DAY 24
Jesus Returns To Galilee

The Sermon on the Mount was, and still is, revolutionary. The truths Jesus revealed changed lives, families, cultures and nations. Jesus taught about this more than once and may have emphasized a different part depending on the audience and His purpose.

The Sermon on the Mount was given on a plain in the mountains overlooking the Sea of Galilee and all the cities that surround it. It is an area known for its remarkable beauty and served as the perfect location for a breathtaking message.

Today we look at the Sermon on the Mount in Luke. Read Luke 6:17-49.
Who was Jesus addressing when He spoke this message?

Note in verses 20-23 what Jesus says will bless us and make us glad. Write down
the person's condition and the promise He gives them.

What are we told to do when people ostracize, scorn and insult us because we
are Christians? Is that hard for you to practice or even fathom?

Who are the "woes" aimed at in verses 24-26? What warning is Jesus giving us?
Does it make sense that when we seek those things, in the end we get none, but
when we seek Him then we get all that really matters?

Now read verses 27-37. What stands out most to you? Which command is the
hardest one for you to obey? Which one is the easiest? Look at verse 31, the
Golden Rule. How does it help fulfill everything that Jesus asks of us?

What stands out to you most looking at verses 39-45? According to verse 40, what is the result of being fully trained or spiritually mature? What are we known by, in verses 44-45?

In verses 46-49, Jesus summed up the Sermon on the Mount in a powerful way. What question did He ask? How would you answer Him? What is the difference between the wise person and the foolish one?

Write a prayer asking the Lord to reveal where you need to grow most to be like Him. Ask Him to strengthen you, enlighten you and guide you to live these amazing truths.

DAY 25
Jesus Returns To Galilee

Today we are going to read the Sermon on the Mount in its entirety. Remember, this is a message that Jesus gave many times. As you read it, imagine what it would have been like to hear Him give this message. Give an example of how He taught with authority.

Read Matthew 5-7.
What stands out to you now that you have read His entire sermon?

How would this message have affected the people who were listening? How does it affect you? Would you have wanted to follow Him after hearing this?

Which part of the message excites you the most?

Which part is hardest for you to enact within your life and why?

Which part would give people the most hope and why?

Before writing your prayer, sit quietly for a minute and ask the Lord to tell you what you should learn from this. As He speaks to you, write it down.

DAY 26
Jesus Returns To Galilee

After giving the Sermon on the Mount, Jesus traveled back to Capernaum. As He entered the town, Jewish leaders approached asking Him to heal the servant of a Centurion. If He agreed, Jesus most likely would go to Tiberius. This Roman city was considered unclean in the Jewish community because it was a capital city of that region and it had a cemetery.

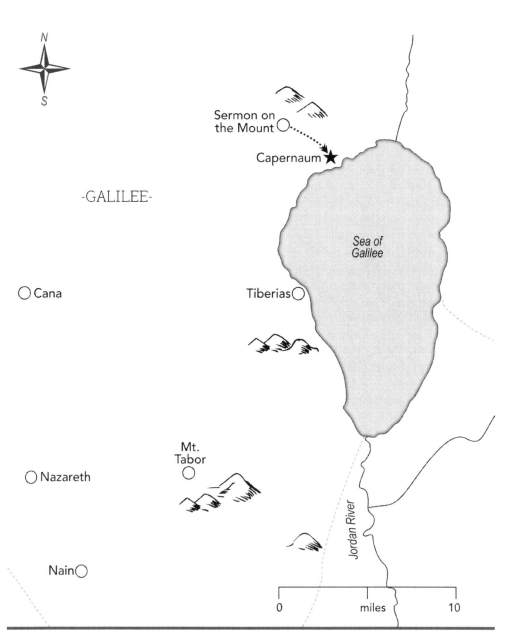

Read Luke 7:1-10. A Roman Centurion was the commander of 100 men. This was an elite and powerful position to hold. What do we know about this man in verses 1-5?

Looking at verses 6-8, what more do we learn about him? What was the Centurion's view of Jesus and His authority?

According to verse 9, what made Jesus marvel? What does this tell you about Jesus and what He values? What do you learn about Jesus from this?

Do you possess this valuable attribute? If so, describe a time you showed it and explain what happend.

Write a prayer asking the Lord to strengthen your faith, making it so strong that Jesus would have noticed. Ask Him to show you ways you can trust Him more. Ask Him to show you how to demonstrate each one.

DAY 27
Jesus Returns To Galilee

From Capernaum, Jesus travelled 25 miles southwest to Nain, which appears to be the only time He visited this city. A large crowd accompanied Him. They did not know that Jesus intended to meet someone whose heart was broken and whose world had fallen apart. He wanted to show love and bring healing.

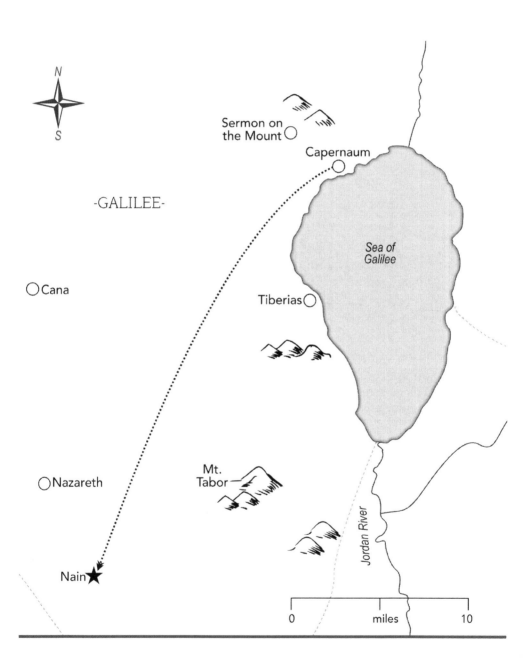

Read Luke 7:11-17.
Looking at verses 11-12, what does Jesus' moment of arrival tell you about Him? In verse 13, how did Jesus feel about what happened?

Note that this mother had lost her only son. Meaning, not only was she childless, but she had no one to take care of her and protect her. Have you ever had a time when you felt like you lost what mattered most and that your world was falling apart? How did you feel? Did you sense that Jesus' heart went out to you?

Looking at verses 14-15, how do you think the mother felt in this moment? How do you think Jesus felt as He did this for her?

What was the reaction of the crowd in verses 16-17? How would you have felt if you witnessed this?

The Greek word for compassion, found in verse 13, means to feel from the deepest depths of your being. It is a strong word that shows great emotion. What does this tell you about Jesus? Meditate on what this says about how He feels for you. Write a prayer praising His compassion for you. Tell Him you know He will only do what is best for you and that you trust in that care.

DAY 28
Jesus Returns To Galilee

John the Baptist had risen up as a great prophet with huge crowds following him. He spoke out for God and prepared the way for Jesus' coming. He baptized Jesus and saw the Holy Spirit descend on Him as a dove. Then, because He openly rebuked Herod who had taken his brother's wife, he was thrown into prison.

It would make sense that sitting in the darkness of the dungeon, he would begin to question what he had seen. But now he was hearing of even greater miracles and more astounding acts of Jesus. So, he sent to find out if everything he had heard was true.

Read Matthew 11:2-19.
In verses 2-3, what was John asking? Why?

How did Jesus respond in verses 4-6?

John knew the prophesies, found in Isaiah 35:3-6 and 61:1-3, of what the coming Messiah would be like. Comparing these with Matthew 11:4-6, what would Jesus' answer have meant to John?

KNOW HIS LOVE AND HEAR HIS VOICE

What do these passages tell you about Jesus?

Read Matthew 7:11-15. What do these verses tell you about John the Baptist? By the way, if you are wondering if John the Baptist was actually Elijah, we will answer that on another day.

For now, read verses 16-19. What is Jesus telling us about pleasing certain people? Can you remember a time when, no matter what you did, there were people who would only say negative things about you? How does this help you relate to Jesus?

What does Jesus say at the end of verse 19? What does this mean?

John wanted to ask Jesus a big question that weighed on his mind. Are there any questions you want Jesus to answer? Write them down and pray for the Lord to bring you the answers.

■LIFE GROUP DISCUSSION QUESTIONS■

DISCUSS THESE QUESTIONS TOGETHER:

1. Read Matthew 12:9-12. Do you see hypocrisy in the way the people were thinking? Have you ever found yourself allowing some things to be "okay" during your Sabbath, giving it a free pass to continue as usual on such a day because it had to do with your business or line of work?

2. In Day 23 of the journal, we listed the names of the Apostles and what we know of each of them. What stood out to you about these men? What would your name be if you were listed in this passage with them?

3. The "beatitudes" of Matthew 5 often speak against cultural norms and common practices in our world. We are told to be gentle, merciful, and peacemakers who are poor in spirit. Read Matthew 5 with your group and discuss what each "beatitude" means. How can you live out each of the 8? What does it mean to say that those who do these things will be the "light" and "salt?"

4. Revisit Day 27 of the journal. Focus on the question about the mother losing her only son. Discuss your answers as a group. Are these struggles of the past or present? Pray for these struggles together as a group.

►LIFE GROUP DISCUSSION QUESTIONS◄

APPLY WHAT YOU'VE LEARNED THIS
WEEK BY PUTTING IT INTO PRACTICE:

LOVE LIKE JESUS

Each beatitude points us toward a service of others. What beatitude can you practice this week? Choose a beatitude and look for the blessing God promises through this.

INTENTIONAL INTIMACY

Read Luke 6:12. What did Jesus do before choosing the twelve Apostles? Be intentional about applying this same practice to situations you face this week. When you catch yourself planning and making things happen without first praying on it, stop yourself. Take the time to wait on the Lord's direction by spending time with Him in prayer and in His word daily.

FULLY SURRENDERED

Do you find yourself saying things like, "If I had that kind of time, I would…" or, "If only I were gifted like that, I could do…" or, "If I had more money, I would…" Read Luke 6:38 and apply it to your life this week. Focus on what you do have and use it to serve the Lord. As you do this, you will see blessings overflow in your life.

EXPERIENCE MORE

This week, ask God to open your eyes to those you can help and care for. Do your best to respond to their needs right away, and don't allow yourself to get caught up in putting it off for a later day.

DAY 29
Jesus Returns To Galilee

Jesus was aware that not everyone would receive Him and His message. Sadly, those who are not open to God and His love will never know the joys of the Kingdom. It is interesting that the city that saw the most miracles is not around today. Geographically, it was the perfect place to live. What led to the devastation of this once beautiful city? Today we see the answer. It is a stark lesson about what can happen to a city, and to an individual, that rejects Jesus.

Start your reading by going back to Matthew 11:16-30.
Looking at verses 20-24, what did Jesus say to the cities He denounced? Why was He so stern? What does this tell you about the Judgment? What does this tell you about Jesus?

Real faith in God is not based on signs and miracles. So, what is the most effective way we can see real faith born?

Now look at verses 25-27. What is Jesus revealing to us about who will come to Him and who will not? Why do some come, while others do not?

In verse 28, who is He inviting?

In verses 28-30, what does Jesus promise He will do for anyone who comes to Him? What are we asked to do? If you are doing this, how has it affected your life?

Billy Graham said, "If God does not judge the United States, He will have to apologize to Sodom and Gomorrah." After the reading today, do you see what Billy Graham was getting at? Explain.

Write a prayer for our country and your city. Pray that we will have eyes and hearts to know who Jesus is. Pray that anyone you know who is weary and carrying a heavy burden will turn to Jesus and find rest for their souls.

DAY 30
Jesus Returns To Galilee

Jesus was called the friend of sinners (Luke 7:34). He was their friend, and the good news is this means He is my friend, too. He cares for all, loves all and has compassion for all. Jesus was strong in His stand against anyone who sought to cast people down, out or aside.

Read Luke 7:36-50.
When people ate a meal back then, they reclined at the table which was low to the ground. Jesus' feet would not have been covered by the table. What happened when the woman came up and anointed his feet? What was Simon's reaction? How would this have made her feel? Why do you think she would do such a thing?

Why did Jesus begin with a parable in verses 40-50? What does that tell you about the best way to go into a time of teaching?

What is the point of the parable? Which one are you, the one forgiven little or the one forgiven much?

Washing a guest's feet was customary to do in that day. Why do you think Simon did not offer to wash Jesus' feet? What does this tell you about his respect for Jesus? What does the woman's actions tell you about her respect for Jesus?

Look at verse 47. Do you believe the parable's lesson is true? Why would this be the case?

When Jesus stood up for the woman, in the way he did, what did you learn about Him?

Write a prayer telling Jesus why you love Him. What does it mean to you that He died for your sins? He is willing to cleanse you completely, forgiving everything you have ever done wrong. How do you feel about that?

DAY 31
Jesus Returns To Galilee

Jesus remains in Galilee, a region known for its rich soil and abundant agriculture. However, like anywhere else, there were places good for farming and places that would yield nothing. From the mountain areas, you could see where it would be successful to plant and where it would not. Jesus uses the landscape around Him to teach a lesson to the people that they would never forget.

Take note, in Mark 4:13, Jesus explains that the parable of the soils is so important that it is the key to understanding all parables!

Read Luke 8:1-15.
In verses 1-3, who was now traveling with Jesus and what are we told about them? What does this say about Jesus' view of women?

Look at Matthew 13:10-17, along with Luke 8:9-10. Why does Jesus teach in parables? What does this say about our personal responsibility to seek, tune-in and understand what God wants us to know?

Jesus tells us there are four kinds of reactions from people who hear the message of the Kingdom of God. As you read each one, think about people you know who have responded in that way.

The Road: Luke 8:11-12 and Matthew 13:19
What is the seed? What happens when these people hear the Word of God? What does this tell you about the Devil and the spiritual warfare that takes place when the Word is shared? Knowing this, how important is it that we pray for people who are going to hear the Word? Who are some people you know that had this reaction and result?

The Rocky Soil: Luke 8:13 and Matthew 13:20-21
What is this person's reaction to hearing the Word and what is the end-result? Did they have initial life and growth? Why did this person not last? What will cause them to eventually turn away? Do you know someone who had this reaction and result?

The Thorns and Weeds: Luke 8:14 and Matthew 13:22
What is this person's reaction to hearing the Word of God? Is there initially life and fruit? What is the end result? What are the things that choke the life out of them? Do you know anyone who had this reaction and result?

The Good Soil: Luke 8:15 and Matthew 13:23
What is this person's reaction to hearing the Word of God? Putting Luke and Matthew together, why do they understand the Word? To remain faithful, how important is understanding? What do they bear fruit with? How much fruit do they bear? Do you know anyone who had this reaction and result?

Why do you think this parable is the key to all parables and to understanding how the message of Jesus works? What does this tell you about Jesus? What does this tell you about you?

Write a prayer asking God to make your heart like the good soil. Ask Him to help you be one who hears the Word and understands it. Pray that God uses you to share with others and pray they will have hearts to hear. Pray for those who are now no longer walking with Jesus and pray their hearts will change.

DAY 32
Jesus Returns To Galilee

Right after Jesus gives the Parable of the Soils, Mark drives home the message with this next section. Here we learn what we are accountable for and are given a warning and a promise. This is a deep section of scripture requiring you to really take the time to study it and apply it to your life.

Read Mark 4:21-29.
Focus on verse 24. What is Jesus telling you to do? How does that apply to the Parable of the Soils that we looked at yesterday?

Now look at and think about verses 21-22. What is Jesus teaching us? Do you feel that you live a transparent life? Are you willing to shine as a light for Him?

Look back at Matthew 5:14-16 and Numbers 32:23. How do these bring more understanding to what we are told in verses 21-22?

Now look and think about verses 24-25. What is Jesus telling us? What is He promising us? What warning does He give us? Do you really want to be one to whom more is given? Why or why not?

Jesus sums up the Parable of the Talents (Bags of Gold) in Matthew 25:29-30. This is where He says the servant who is faithful will be rewarded and get more. The servant who is not faithful will go into punishment and have everything taken away. How does this align with what Jesus taught?

Do you see, even more, how Jesus taught with authority? Write a prayer to the Lord understanding and explaining that He knows everything about what you say, do and think. Ask Him to give you the wisdom and strength to live a transparent life. Ask Him to make you one who hears and understands. Ask Him to show you how you can serve faithfully.

DAY 33
Jesus Returns To Galilee

Jesus began His ministry in conflict with the Devil and it did not end there. In the Parable of the Tares and the Wheat, Jesus warns us of the enemy's strategy. It is vital that we know we are in a war and the enemy has planted some of his followers in our midst.

To understand this parable it will help to know that tares are weeds that look like wheat when they first sprout up. As they grow, their true identity becomes more obvious. In the end they bear no fruit, only destruction. Tares are insidious in that they wrap their roots around the wheat, so when you attempt to pull them up they will take some of the wheat with them.

Read Matthew 13:24-30 and 36-43.
Write down each person mentioned in verses 36-43. Note who they are and what they do.

Key in on verse 41 and pay specific attention to how the tares cause hurt and pain within the Church. Have you seen this happen? How does this affect the way those outside the Church view us?

Look at Matthew 18:1-7. What does this tell you about stumbling blocks?

Read 2 Corinthians 11:13-15. How does this fit with what Jesus tells us in the parable?

Now look at 1 Corinthians 11:19. What does this tell you must happen and why?

Look back at Matthew 13:43 and also read Daniel 12:3. What does this tell you about the members of the Church that are truly committed to Christ?

Knowing that there must be those within the Church who are not for the Church, write a prayer asking God to protect those who are new in their faith from being discouraged. Ask God to help keep you focused on the good. Pray that you will have insight and will be able to spot those who are not true Christ-followers.

DAY 34
Jesus Returns To Galilee

Jesus wants us to know that His kingdom will grow fast and spread wide. He uses the small mustard seed as an illustration. To the people of that day, the mustard seed was known as the smallest of all seeds. They are so small that it is hard to see one with the naked eye. Yet, once it is planted, it will grow 12 to 15 feet high in a single season. The mustard plant also spreads quickly, yielding not just one plant, but a colony of mustard plants, filling the surrounding area. The people Jesus taught would have known all of this.

Read Matthew 13:31-35 and 44-52.
What do these parables have in common? What do they teach you about the Kingdom of God?

What did you learn about the Kingdom of God from the Parable of the Mustard seed? Birds were often a sign of something bad. Thinking back to the Parable of the Wheat and the Tares, what does Jesus want us to know?

Look at verse 44-46. What is Jesus telling us about the Kingdom of God? What are these people willing to give to possess the Kingdom of God? What motivates these men? Do you feel this way about being with Jesus and having His Lordship active in your life?

Reading verses 47-50, what does Jesus tell us about the Church and what will happen at the end of the age? How does this describe the Church right now? How does this fit with the Parable of the Wheat and the Tares?

In verses 51-52, Jesus asks if we have understood all of this. Have you? Do you think you understand what He wants you to know about the Kingdom of God (His Church)? What did you learn? Why is this important?

Matthew 13:52 (NASB) - And Jesus said to them, *"Therefore every scribe who has become a disciple of the kingdom of heaven is like a head of a household, who brings out of his treasure things new and old."* A scribe was an expert in the Old Testament. What did Jesus say will happen when a scribe comes into the Kingdom of God? Is the Old Testament to be cast aside or treasured along with the New?

Ask Jesus to help you understand the Kingdom and how this applies to your life. Write a prayer telling God that you will give all and give anything to be with Him. Ask Him to bless your Church, causing it to grow rapidly.

DAY 35
Jesus Returns To Galilee

Huge crowds were now flocking around Jesus. Even his own mother and brothers found it difficult to get to Him.

Read Matthew 12:46-50 and Luke 8:19-21.
Jesus was told His mother and brothers were outside. How did He respond? How do you think the crowd reacted to His statements?

What is true of those who have a very real and genuine relationship with Him? How would they act and what would they be doing? Is this true of you?

How close are we with Jesus if we are truly His? Does it make you stop and think about the kind of relationship He wants with you?

Write a prayer asking Jesus to draw you closer to Him. Tell Him how you feel about Him. Ask Him to help you sense His presence more clearly and to be more in tune with His voice and desires.

■ LIFE GROUP DISCUSSION QUESTIONS ■

DISCUSS THESE QUESTIONS TOGETHER:

1. Read Matthew 7:16-19. What is a "good tree?" What do "trees" have to do with people in this scripture? What is Jesus telling us about people? Would you consider yourself a good or bad tree?

2. How many of you feel that you carry the weight of the world on your shoulders? Are you weighed down by the financial stresses of your household, or your health, or the health of your loved ones? Read Matthew 11:28-30 to see how Jesus tells us to find rest. Take time to share the "weights" you're carrying this week with your group. Pray over one another and lay each of your burdens at the foot of the cross.

3. Jesus tells us why He speaks in parables in Matthew 13:10-17. How does His explanation apply to us today?

4. Each of us has encountered various stumbling blocks in our life. Scripture is very clear on what we are to do with them. It also tells us to be cautious so that we are not another person's stumbling block. Read Matthew 18:1-9. What action does this call you to in your personal life?

5. In Day 34 of the journal, we read Matthew 13:31-35 and 44-52. What are the parables He taught? What did you take away from the passages regarding the Church? Why is this important?

►LIFE GROUP DISCUSSION QUESTIONS◄

APPLY WHAT YOU'VE LEARNED THIS
WEEK BY PUTTING IT INTO PRACTICE:

LOVE LIKE JESUS

What do we know of those who are in a genuine relationship with the Lord? Is it evident that those people love the Lord? Would it be fair to say that their love for the Lord overflows to others? How can you live such a life this week so that others will see you as being in true relationship with Christ by the way you love?

INTENTIONAL INTIMACY

The places we find ourselves and the things we fill our time with are vital to our walk with Christ. Read Matthew 13:22 and Luke 8:14 to see what can happen when we're not careful. What warning can you heed from these passages?

FULLY SURRENDERED

Jesus is very clear about the results of our generosity. What does Matthew 25:29-30 tell you to expect when you have surrendered your time, talent and treasure to the Lord? What does it say of the contrary?

EXPERIENCE MORE

A mustard seed, a seed known to be smaller than all other seeds, is a plant that grows and overtakes its surroundings. How could something as small as a mustard seed become the largest presence in a garden? How could a small act of faith cause your faith to grow beyond imagination?

DAY 36
Jesus Returns To Galilee

It appears that after Mary and His brothers sought Jesus, He then returned to His hometown of Nazareth where he had grown up and had a career as a carpenter. There, Jesus revealed He was the Messiah they had been longing for. While they knew He did miracles, for some reason, the majority could not see Him in this new light. Sadly, the people of Nazareth could have seen and experienced so much, yet something kept them from it. Hopefully, that will not be true of you.

Read Matthew 13:53-58 and Mark 6:1-6.
What was the people's reaction to Jesus in Mark 6:1-2? What was it that made such a huge impression? What did you learn about Jesus from this? What was He like? Were the people aware of His miracles?

Now focus on Mark 6:3-4. What kept the people who knew Him all of His life from believing that He is the Messiah? Do you think there are many who sense the power and presence of Jesus but explain it away because it does not align with what they think is true?

How do you think this made Jesus feel?

When Jesus said a "prophet is not without honor, except in his hometown and among his relatives" does that give us a warning about how we treat those who grow up in our Church? What about in your family? How can we prevent this from happening?

Look at Matthew 13:58. Read it over a few times. What is this saying? How tightly are Jesus' miracles based on your trust in Him? What does this tell you about faith and seeing the hand of God move?

Write a prayer asking God to cleanse you of any doubts and disbelief. Tell Him you want to see His power and promises enacted in your life. Ask Him to make your faith one He marvels at and not wonders about.

DAY 37
Jesus Returns To Galilee

Jesus is now sending the 12 out again. In Mark 3:13-19, He chose the 12 then sent them to be trained. Now they are to spread the message of the Kingdom of God and to magnify the effect of Jesus' message and methods.

Read Mark 6:7-13.
Why is it significant that Jesus sent them out in pairs? What does that tell you about the most effective way to minister and live life?

Jesus repeated the same instructions He gave when sending them out the first time. What does that tell you about the need for a leader to keep the message constant and clear? What do you learn from Jesus' leadership style?

What message did the Apostles share when they went out? Why this message? Is the Church supposed to have the same message when we go out?

Look at verses 14-16. What was Herod's reaction? How did the people who heard about the Apostles react? It is important to note that Herod and the people pointed to Jesus, even though the Apostles were sharing the message and doing works. When the Church goes out, should we get the same result?

Read Mark 6:30-32. What did Jesus do when they came back from their mission? How would this apply to your life?

Write a prayer asking the Lord to show you your mission. Ask Him to tell you the works He wants you to do. Pray He will show you who to partner with so that you may be even more effective. Pray that as you live out His plan for your life, He will get the glory.

DAY 38
Jesus Returns To Galilee

John the Baptist made a huge impact for Jesus. He came with powerful preaching and a lifestyle that captivated the crowds.

Read Mark 6:14-29.
Why did Herod have John arrested? How did Herod feel about him? What major character flaws do we see in Herod?

Read Matthew 11:7-15.
What does Jesus tell us about John?

Look at verse 14. Jesus says that "if" you are willing to accept it, John is Elijah who "is" to come. While Jesus is saying that Elijah is still to come, John has already come in the spirit of Elijah. Jesus was addressing a belief that Elijah had to return before the Messiah would come, based on Malachi 4:5-6.

The people did not know that the Messiah would come and be killed, then He would rise from the dead and return. Elijah would come before the second coming. So, Jesus is telling them that if you need to see Elijah before accepting me, then John should fulfill that desire.

Read Matthew 17:10-13. What is Jesus telling us about Elijah and John the Baptist?

Read 1:6-8 and verses 19-28.
What was John's mission? Who did he say he was and who did he say he was not?

As you think about what you learned today, what stands out most? For sure, we see that John was faithful to the end. Write a prayer asking God to cause you to be faithful every day of your life. Ask the Lord if you have unknown character flaws and to give you guidance and strength to overcome them.

DAY 39
Jesus Returns To Galilee

When the Apostles returned from their mission they were excited to spend time with Jesus. They wanted to share with Him what they had accomplished. Jesus wanted quality time with them too, but also knew how much they needed rest.

Jesus now shows the fourth sign that John said would reveal Jesus as the Messiah and how He works in our lives.

Read John 6:1-14 and Mark 6:30-32.
Where did Jesus want them to go and why?

Read Mark 6:33-44.
In verses 33-34, why did Jesus choose to be with the crowd instead of spending time alone with the Apostles? What does this tell you about Jesus?

Look again at verses 35-38. What does Jesus ask the Apostles to do? What is their response? Why does He ask them what they have? What does this tell you about how Jesus wants to work with us and with what we have?

How did Jesus organize the people in verses 39-40? What does this tell you about Jesus and His leadership? How important was it for Jesus to organize the people before performing the miracle? What would have gone wrong if He did not?

What did Jesus do in verses 41-44, and what was the result? How important is prayer to our seeing God; how does it cause things to occur beyond our resources and abilities?

How did the people react, according to John 6:14?

What does the feeding of the 5,000 tell us about Jesus and how He works in our lives?

Write a prayer asking the Lord to show you what you have and what He wants you to do with it. Commit to be completely obedient. Ask Him what He will do beyond all you ask or think.

DAY 40
Jesus Returns To Galilee

After the feeding of the 5,000, Jesus was ready to show His Disciples the fifth sign that showed He was the Messiah.

Read John 6:15-24.
Now look at Mark 6:45-46 and John 6:15. Why did Jesus make the Disciples get in the boat and leave? What did He do after they left?

Read John 6:18 and Mark 6:47-48. What was Jesus doing? What problem did the disciples face? Was Jesus aware of what was happening?

Focus on John 6:19-21 and Mark 6:48-50. Write down what happened. What did Jesus say to them? What were they supposed to have learned from this? How important is it to note that Jesus would have passed them by if they had not invited Him in?

In John 6:20, Jesus literally says the words, "I AM." In Hebrew, this would have been the Holy Name of God. It can be found in Exodus 3:14. What is Jesus saying to them? Why would this be a reason to be afraid more than ever?

In Mark 6:51-52, what was the reaction of the Apostles? What were they missing and why? Jesus was patient with them and willing to give them time to learn; what does that say about how He will deal with you?

Have you had a time when you thought the Lord sent you into a storm to learn a lesson? What happened?

Write a prayer telling the Lord that you trust Him with the storms and challenges you will face in life. Invite Him to be with you and teach you in the midst of the storms.

DAY 41
Jesus Returns To Galilee

Jesus had prepared the Apostles for the storms that would come. Now that test is going to be put to good use. They had seen the crowds growing; Jesus' popularity was at an all-time high. The crowds, however, consisted of consumers not followers. When he fed them they were ecstatic. When He called them to follow and be committed, they were offended.

Read John 6:22-7:1.
In verses 22-25, what did the crowds notice? When they sought for Jesus, where did they go? Why is Capernaum important? What did we learn on Day 29 concerning Jesus' warnings to Capernaum?

Focus on verses 26-27. What did Jesus tell the people about themselves? Could He say that about you? What does He tell them to do and why?

In verses 28-29 we are told what the true work of God is. What is it? How does that fit with what Jesus has already said? What does it mean for you to do the true work of God? How would that be lived out in your life, every day?

In verses 30-34 the people ask Jesus for something. What was it? If they really believed in Him, would they ask Him to do their will or would they want to do His will?

Pay close attention to verses 35-40. What did Jesus promise? What problem kept the people from receiving the promise? What did they seek and what should they have sought instead? How did Jesus live His life and what was His purpose? What is the will of God?

What stands out to you in verses 41-51? What was Jesus' warning and what did He promise to those who have hearts set on the right thing?

In verses 52-57, the people had a problem with what Jesus is saying. Did Jesus seek to appease them or call for an all-out commitment? Why did he do it in this way? What does this tell you about Jesus' values and what He wants from you?

This conflict reaches a climax in verses 59-66. Where did Jesus have this confrontation? What do you remember about the man who headed this Synagogue from Day 15 of this journal? Knowing that most of the Jesus' miracles were done in this place, what can you determine is happening?

In verses 6:60-71, we see one of the most touching moments in all of the Bible. The crowds had left and Jesus was with the Apostles. What did He ask them? How did Peter respond? How do you think Jesus felt in this moment? What does this tell you about the Apostles' commitment? Are you that committed to Jesus?

Write a prayer telling the Lord that you would follow Him no matter what. Tell Him that you love Him, trust Him and will always follow Him. If you cannot write that prayer, then ask Him to help you come to the place of true commitment.

DAY 42

After this intense situation, Jesus traveled 35 miles to the coastal city of Tyre. As far as we know, this is the only time that Jesus went to this area.

Read Mark 7:24-30. Now let's look at Matthew's account by reading Matthew 15:21-23. What was the issue the mother was hoping Jesus would free her daughter from? What does her persistence say about her faith? How does this apply to the way you pray?

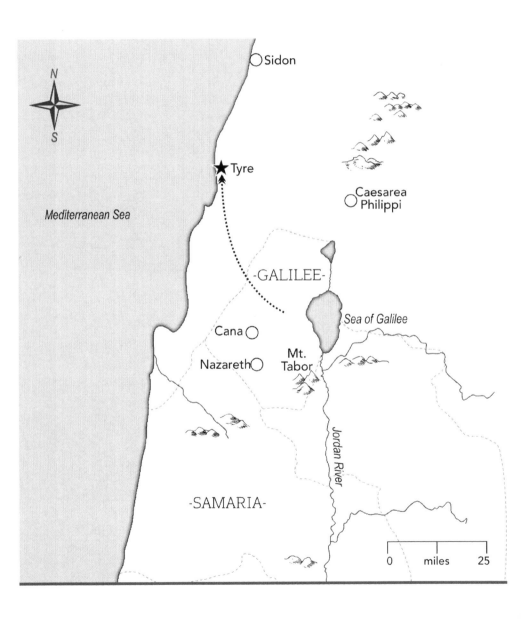

What did Jesus tell her in Matthew 15:24 and Mark 7:27? Why do you think Jesus responded in this way?

What was the mother's response according to Mark 7:28-30 and Matthew 15:27-28? What did Jesus say her response showed? What was the result of her persistent faith?

What does this tell you about what Jesus values? How passionate does Jesus want us to be in our prayers? Look at Matthew 5:7-11 and Luke 18:1-8. How do these passages apply to what we just studied?

Write a prayer for something that you really want Jesus to handle. What is it that you are begging Him for? Tell Him why this is important to you.

■ LIFE GROUP DISCUSSION QUESTIONS ■

DISCUSS THESE QUESTIONS TOGETHER:

1. What keeps us from experiencing "miracles?" Read Matthew 13:53-58 and Mark 6:1-6. Do you see miracles happening around you? If not, why do you think you're not witnessing such things?

2. It's easy to find ourselves discounting those we interact with on a regular basis. We can lose the marvel of what we have when we allow ourselves to become "used to it." How can we prevent this from happening in our church, homes, and place of work?

3. Five loaves of bread and two fish fed 5,000 men and their families. What caused that small amount of food to feed so many men? Read Mark 6:33-44. What is the Lord asking you to bring before Him so that He can multiply it? How does this make you feel about having enough where you are today?

4. Read John 6:18 and Mark 6:47-48. Why were the disciples worried and afraid? Where was Jesus? Was He unaware of the troubles they were facing? What does this tell you about the troubles you face?

APPLY WHAT YOU'VE LEARNED THIS
WEEK BY PUTTING IT INTO PRACTICE:

LOVE LIKE JESUS

Jesus sent His disciples out in pairs. Why did He do this? As a group, plan a time to go out and perform acts of kindness or service around the community.

INTENTIONAL INTIMACY

Mark 7:28-30 and Matthew 15:27-28 show us a woman who is desperate to see her daughter freed from the possession of a demon. She repeatedly comes before Jesus begging for her daughter's freedom. She is intentional to place herself before Him and make her requests known, while maintaining a great faith in His abilities. Be intentional with God this week. Make coming before Him a daily practice.

FULLY SURRENDERED

How do the various serving teams at Crossroads serve the mission of Jesus?

EXPERIENCE MORE

In John 6:30-34, the people ask Jesus for a sign to prove that He is who He says He is. Their faith is contingent on a "miraculous sign." What sign have you been asking God to perform in order for you to serve Him outside of your comfort zone? This week, take the conditions off of your "experience more" and choose a place to serve others!

DAY 43

After spending a short time in the region of Tyre and Sidon, Jesus makes his way back to Galilee.

Read Matthew 15:29-39.
What did Jesus do according to verses 29-31?

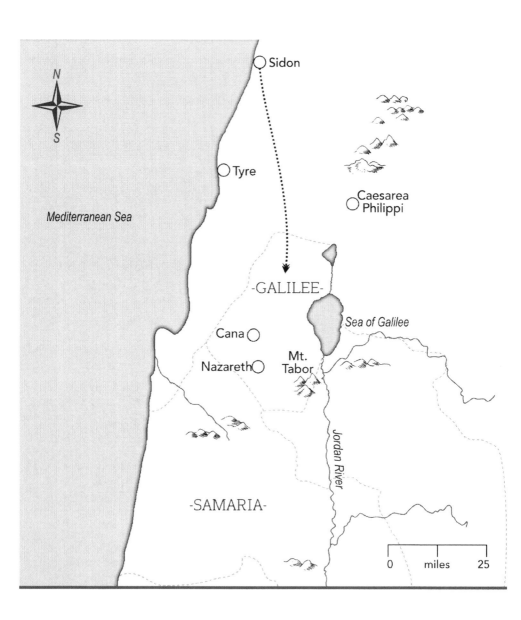

Look at verse 32. How long did Jesus minister to this group of people? How did Jesus feel about them? How important was it to Jesus to meet their physical needs? What did He tell the Apostles He wanted to do?

Are you surprised at the Apostles' response in verse 33? Look back at Mark 6:51-52. What does that tell you about why they responded this way?

What happened according to verses 34-39? How many loaves and fish did Jesus use to do this miracle? How many people did He feed? How many loaves and fish did Jesus use to feed the 5,000 (Mark 6:38)? Why did Jesus use different amounts to get different results? Is there a vital truth to learn from this?

Write a prayer asking Jesus to use you. Ask Him to show your part in His mission. Pray that you will have a heart that is sensitive to what He is doing and wants to do.

DAY 44
Jesus Returns To Galilee

Jesus is still in the Galilean region. He is about half-way into His ministry with the Apostles. Now it is time for Him to bring understanding to what He has been doing and what they have been seeing. The next three events will open their eyes in a big way.

Read Matthew 16:1-12.
Looking at verses 1-6. What did the Pharisees and Sadducees want? How did Jesus answer?

Both groups were experts in the Old Testament and Jesus was fulfilling prophecy after prophecy right before their eyes. How does that bring a deeper understanding to this exchange?

They were able to discern the signs in their day; are you aware of the signs in ours?

Look at verses 5-7. What did Jesus say to the Apostles and what was their response?

In verses 8-12, Jesus brought understanding to what He had been telling them and what they had seen. What was Jesus teaching them? Looking at Mark 8:16-21, what answers did they give to each of His questions. What lesson did He want them to learn and what did He want them to understand?

Write a prayer asking the Lord to give you a mind to understand and a heart to know the deep truths He wants to reveal to you. Ask Him to open your eyes to discern the times you live in.

JESUS TRAVELS TO CAESAREA PHILIPPI

DAY 45

Jesus left the region of the Sea of Galilee for a 30-mile journey, a 14-hour walk, to Caesarea Philippi. The Bible only records Him traveling there on this one occasion. This place provided Him with a dramatic backdrop to unveil that He is the Christ, the Son of the Living God. It was in Caesarea Philippi that Jesus chose to inaugurate His Church and declare the Church's power and mission. Upon this rock I will build My church, and the gates of Hell will not overpower it (Matthew 16:18 NASB).

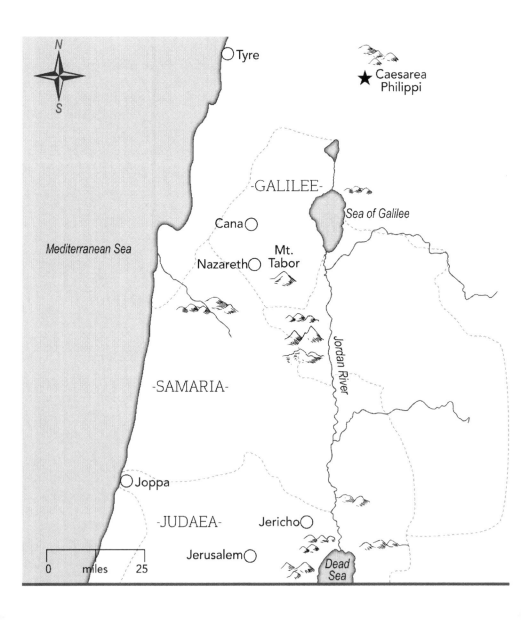

Caesarea Philippi was a Roman city built on and against a huge, majestic rock formation. It was a popular place for false worship and hedonistic celebrations. At one time, the city was called Paneas, after the Greek god, Pan. His temple was built at the mouth of a dark and immense cave; this is also where sacrifices were made. Pan was worshipped as the God of panic who would bring military victory by causing fear (panic) in the enemy. Pan was also a god of sexuality and wine. He was thought to be one of the few gods who could cross into Hades and return.

Jesus intentionally chose Caesarea Phillipi as the place to reveal His identity, His plan to die upon the Cross, and the Church, which would be born from His sacrifice. The dark cave, with its cultic practices, would be a visual representation of the gate of Hades. The rock formation, on which the Temples were built, would graphically drive home His message.

Read Matthew 16:13-28.
In verses 13-14, what question did Jesus ask and what was the initial response? What did Jesus want them to know?

In verses 15-19, Jesus made the question personal. How did Peter answer? What did he mean? According to Jesus, how did Peter know this?

What is the "Rock" that Jesus would build His Church on? What does Jesus say about His Church? Why do you think Jesus chose this place to reveal the truth?

Keys are a sign of responsibility, trust and leadership. When your parents gave you the keys to the car, what statement were they making? What would it mean if someone gave you the keys to their house? So, what is Jesus saying when He tells Peter He is giving him the keys to the Kingdom? What does this say about Apostolic authority?

Jesus shared His plan with the Apostles in verse 21. What is Jesus' mission?

In Luke 9:22, Jesus tells us what He "must" do. What is it?

How did Peter react to this message in Matthew 16:22? Why do you think Peter felt that way?

How did Jesus respond to Peter in verse 23? Where did Jesus say Peter's message was really coming from? How could Peter go from speaking the thoughts of the Holy Spirit to espousing the mind of the Devil? Do you sometimes find yourself thinking one way and then another?

After Jesus told the Apostles who He is and what He was going to do, He revealed the cost of being His disciples. In verses 24-28, what does He say must be true if we are going to follow Him? What happens if we are not willing to give all for Jesus?

How has this been true for you? Are you willing to give all to the Lord? Are you someone who sets your mind on God's interest and not your own?

Write a prayer telling Jesus that you know He is the Christ, the Son of God. Share your commitment to living completely for Him, giving all to Him. Ask Him to make you so discerning that you can distinguish the Holy Spirit from other thoughts that enter your mind.

DAY 46

Jesus ends His time with the Apostles in Caesarea Philippi, where he unveiled the truth of who He is. He told them that some would not taste death till they saw the Son of Man come to His Kingdom. To fulfill this promise, a few days later Jesus took the Apostles to Mount Tabor.

Matthew and Mark said it took six days to get there. Luke said it was "some eight days later." Matthew and Mark explained that they traveled from the time they ended their teaching at Caesarea Philippi. Luke included the time they spent in Caesarea Philippi.

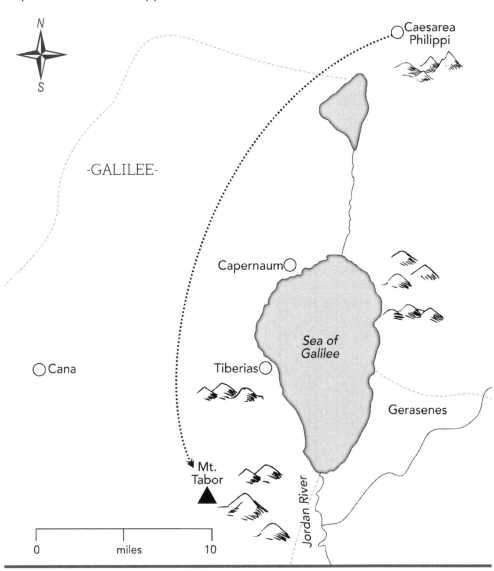

Once they arrived at Mount Tabor, Jesus took Peter, James and John to have a true mountain top experience.

Read Luke 9:27-42.
Looking at Luke 9:28-31, what did Jesus take them up the mountain to do? What happened while they were supposed to be praying? Who was with Jesus? What were they talking about?

The word "departure," in verse 31, is the Greek word "exodos." Why is it significant that Moses spoke to Jesus about His exodus? How does their conversation relate to the purpose Jesus revealed to the Apostles in Caesarea Philippi?

Look at verse 32. Why did Peter, James and John almost miss out on this moment? After walking from Caesarea Philippi to Mount Tabor and then hiking up the mountain, it would make sense that they were worn out. What does this tell you about Jesus' stamina and strength?

Read verses 33-36. What did Peter say he wanted to do? Why would this have been wrong? What does God the Father say to them and to us?

Are you someone who really listens to what God is telling you? What are some of your own examples?

Look at Luke 9:37-42. What happened the day after they came down the mountain? What was waiting for them? What would you expect to see if you came down the mountain with Jesus?

Jesus shares what is needed for us to have victory when we face the enemy. What does He tell us in Matthew 17:19-21?

Write a prayer asking God to speak to you and also promise you will listen to Him. Ask Him to show you things and make your mind sharp in times of prayer. Thank Him for having grace in your moments of weakness.

DAY 47

Jesus now returns to Galilee and to His home in Capernaum. For Jesus, every moment and every situation was an opportunity to teach something new and important.

Read Mark 9:30-32 and Matthew 17:21-23.
What did Jesus say and what was their reaction to His message?

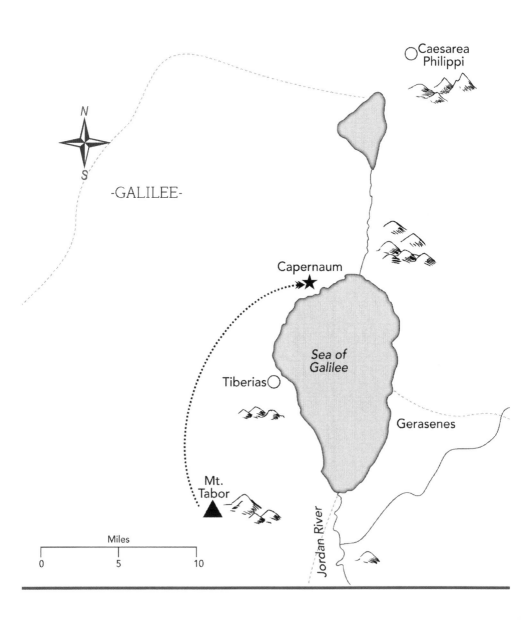

Read Matthew 17:24-27. When they entered Capernaum, what were they supposed to do? What did Jesus tell Peter to do and why? What does this tell you about Jesus?

What does this tell you about how Jesus will work with you in your life?

What were the Disciples discussing in Mark 9:33-36? What was their ambition? What did Jesus teach them? How was the child a perfect lesson for this? Who could you serve and put ahead of yourself?

What did John tell Jesus in Mark 9:38-41? How did Jesus answer and what did He promise? What does that tell you about the need for unity in the Church despite our differences?

Jesus gave a series of strong warnings in verses 42-50. What is He warning against? How should we protect ourselves? Is there anything in your life that needs to be cut off or cut out? Why is it vital to take action and remove it?

At the end of verse 50, Jesus summed-up his teaching moment. What was He saying?

Write a prayer asking the Lord to reveal things only He can show you. Then, ask Him to expose anything in your life that needs to be removed. Ask Him to give you the wisdom and resolve to remove it.

DAY 48
Jesus Returns To Galilee

Jesus has been sharing what He "must" do with His disciples. This mission is the passion of His life; it will steer Him to Jerusalem and to the cross. In Luke 15, He shares how passionate He is for those who are lost, as we should all be.

Read Luke 15.
Looking at verses 1-2, what caused Jesus to share these three parables? What did the Pharisees accuse Him of? What if the world accused the Church of this? How could we do this and do this well?

Read verses 3-7 again. How much is the Shepherd willing to risk for one lost sheep? What does that say about the importance of the one? What does that say about how important you are?

What does the Shepherd do when He realizes a sheep is missing? What is the reaction when He finds it? What is the point Jesus is making?

In the days of Jesus, every Shepherd knew their sheep by name. Knowing this, what does the teaching mean to you?

Read verses 8-10.
In Jesus' day, it was common for a woman to receive coins as a gift from her family in case of financial crisis. These coins were for safety, but they were also considered to be precious gifts from those who loved her.

What did the woman do when she realized one coin was lost? It is highly likely she will burn more oil than the coin is worth. Does that matter to her? Is it a waste? What does that say about the extravagant acts a Church should go to so we can reach the lost? How much is one lost soul worth?

Now Jesus shares the third parable to drive home His point in verses 11-32. What did the younger son do in verses 11-13? What is the result of his actions?

What caused the son to return to the Father in verses 17-19? What was his plan?

According to verse 20, what was the Father's reaction? Write down exactly what the Father did. Do you see that God feels this way about you? Do you get excited knowing that God feels this way about others?

In verses 21-23, what did the son say to the father and what was the father's reaction? Will the father approve of the son being a slave in his home? Did the father make the son go through a time of penance and restitution? Did the father berate the son for his foolishness? What does this tell you about Jesus?

In verses 25-32, Jesus clearly stated that the older brother was like the Pharisees at the beginning of this chapter. How did the older brother react when his younger brother came home? What do you think the older brother believed his younger brother deserved?

What did the father say he had to do when His son returned in verse 32? In all three parables, what emotion is felt when the lost are found? Can you relate to this same emotion?

Write a prayer thanking God for the way He feels about you. Pray for people you know that still need to come to Jesus. Pray your Church is a place that would do anything and spare no expense to see lost people found.

DAY 49
Jesus Returns To Galilee

Restoration and redemption is always the goal of Jesus. When you understand this, you understand the very heart of the Father. Jesus teaches this in a very powerful and practical way.

Read Matthew 18:11-35.
In verses 11-14, what did Jesus say He has come to do? What emotion does He have when His purpose is fulfilled? What is not the will of the Father?

Knowing that restoration and redemption is always the goal, Jesus now teaches in a very personal and practical way. Read verses 15-20. What did Jesus say we should do when someone fails? In verse 15, what are the two things he says you are to do? How important is it that you do this privately?

When you take this first step towards redemption and reconciliation in private, how many other people are supposed to be involved? Why is it that very few people follow what Jesus says here?

If you are not successful, does Jesus tell us to give up? What is the next step in verse 16? What is the purpose of going to this next level?

Read verses 17-20. What does Jesus say the ultimate step should be when we have a Christian brother or sister not willing to leave a sinful lifestyle? What does "bound on earth is bound in heaven" mean? How does "a gathering of two or three in His name" apply to seeking restoration and redemption?

In verses 21-35 Jesus gets even more practical. How often are we to forgive? What happens when we do not forgive? When Jesus has forgiven you for everything, is there anything you should not be willing to forgive?

What would happen if we all followed Jesus' teaching here? What does this tell you about Jesus?

Ask God to reveal someone you should go to who is seeking restoration and forgiveness. Write a prayer asking Him to bring healing and redemption. Pray for anyone else who struggles with forgiveness.

■LIFE GROUP DISCUSSION QUESTIONS ■

DISCUSS THESE QUESTIONS TOGETHER:

1. Read Matthew 16:17-19. What is the "Rock" that Jesus would build His Church on? What does the word "Church" mean in this passage? What confidence does this passage give you about the church body you are meeting with?

2. Do you find it difficult to discern the source of words when talking with others? What did Jesus say about the source of Peter's words in Matthew 16:23? Why was Peter a trap and how can we try to avoid such a trap?

3. When did Jesus become "real" to you? Was that the same time you experienced transformation in your life? If not, when did that happen for you and how? Read Luke 9:27-42 to hear about how Jesus was transformed before Peter, John and James.

4. A church body is made up of many different and unique individuals. As brothers and sisters in Christ, we are to be in unity because of the ultimate commonality: Jesus Christ our Lord and Savior. Mark 9:38-41 emphasizes our need for unity. How are you and your LIFE Group striving to see unity within your community (LIFE Group, church body, churches nationally and internationally)?

5. When a single sheep has gone astray, a shepherd will pursue the lost of his flock. What must that say about the importance of the one sheep to the shepherd? What does it mean to you to be loved by the Shepherd? Read Luke 15:1-2.

▰LIFE GROUP DISCUSSION QUESTIONS▰

APPLY WHAT YOU'VE LEARNED THIS
WEEK BY PUTTING IT INTO PRACTICE:

LOVE LIKE JESUS

How seriously did Jesus take the physical needs of others? Read Matthew 15:32. This week, as a group, make a donation to "the least of these" through our Food Pantry. Items can be dropped off to the church office during normal business hours or placed in the food drums around campus on the weekends.

INTENTIONAL INTIMACY

Be intentional in prayer this week. Ask the Lord to give you a mind and heart to know the things He wishes to reveal to you. Pray for discernment in the times we are living in.

FULLY SURRENDERED

In Matthew 16:24-28, Jesus tells us how to be a disciple of His. Being a disciple of Christ is a daily surrender. What cross have you been hesitant to take up for His namesake? What have you deemed as more valuable than your own soul?

EXPERIENCE MORE

How can we help ministries that serve the "lost or hurting" in our area?

DAY 50

Jesus is going to Jerusalem for the Feast of the Tabernacles. It was a joyous celebration when people would camp out in "booths," usually made of palm branches. People who journeyed to Jerusalem would camp when they arrived. People who lived in Jerusalem would gather on the rooftops with their children, telling stories and eating fun foods. They used this time to remember God's miracles in the wilderness, where the Israelites wandered, before entering the Promised Land.

Read John 7:1-10.
What were Jesus' brothers saying to Him and why? What were they challenging Him to do? How do you think Jesus felt when His own brothers hoped that He would go and be killed?

What was Jesus' response to them? Many older manuscripts used the word "yet" in verse 8. In other words, Jesus never said he was not going to the Feast. He said He was not going "yet." Why would Jesus not go to the Feast with them?

According to verses 11-13, what were the different opinions about Jesus?

Read verses 14-18. What was the reaction when people heard Jesus teach? What does this tell you about Him? What did Jesus say about His own teaching?

Jesus now reveals the truth in a powerful way and He is ready to confront their hypocrisy. Look at verses 19-24. Everyone knew that the leaders were seeking to kill Jesus, so why did they claim they were not?

A person was allowed to be circumcised on the Sabbath but not healed. What does this tell you about their hypocrisy? What does this tell you about what God really values? What is Jesus calling for us to do in verse 24?

Read verses 25-39. Why could no one arrest Jesus? What does Jesus say about where He will soon be going? What does Jesus promise on the last day of the Feast?

What does this mean for you? Do you thirst for what Jesus has for you?

What did the people who were sent to arrest Jesus say about Him in verse 46?

What stands out most to you about Jesus while he was at the Feast of the Tabernacles?

Write a prayer asking Jesus to fill you with the Holy Spirit. Pray that you experience rivers of living water, thirsting for nothing else.

DAY 51
Jesus Journeys To Jerusalem

When the Feast of the Tabernacles came to an end, the religious leaders were plotting every way they could to take Jesus down. They decided that if He were to uphold the Law of Moses by calling for a person to be killed, He would be arrested by the Romans because only Roman officials could call for capital punishment. If He did not uphold the Law of Moses, He would be guilty of breaking the Old Testament Law. He could not be considered the Messiah, hence losing the respect of the people.

So, early the next day at Temple Mount, they attempted to bait Him into their trap.

Read John 8:1-11.
According to verses 1-2, where was Jesus the night before? What did He do when He arrived at the Temple? What does this tell you about how He lived His life?

Read verses 3-6. What did they say about the woman? Why did they bring her to Jesus?

Look at Leviticus 20:10 and Deuteronomy 22:22. What did the Law say regarding adultery? If the woman was caught in the very act, where was the man she was with? Did the Law say she should be put to death or that they should both be put to death? Why do you think Jesus did not argue with them over the fact they did not bring the man? What should we learn from this?

Read verses 6-9 again. Why do you think Jesus wrote on the ground? What do you think He wrote? What did He say about the right to throw the first stone? What was the result of this statement?   If everyone left and Jesus was alone with her, then where were the Apostles? Is it possible they had stones in their hands?

How does this situation apply to our lives?

What did Jesus ask the woman in verses 10-11? What did He call her to do from this point on? What does this tell you about Jesus? How can you apply this to your life?

Write a prayer thanking Jesus for not condemning you. Ask Him to make you one who will not condemn others. Ask Him to bring to mind any sins in your life that you need to put an end to. Pray you can show love to others the way He does.

DAY 52
Jesus Journeys To Jerusalem

The same day Jesus had forgiven the woman caught in adultery, He taught in the Temple. The Pharisees interrupted Him, seeking to put an end to His teaching and ministry. Jesus had not only silenced the Pharisees, He humiliated them. They already hated Him, so they would now use every opportunity to attack Him.

Read John 8:12-59. This is a long section, but keep in mind this all happened in one encounter.

What does Jesus tell us in verse 12? What does He say about Himself? What promise does He make to us if we will follow Him? What does this look like in your life; is this true of you?

Looking at verses 13-19, what was the Pharisees' challenge? Remember, the Law did require two witnesses, as they had mentioned before. How did Jesus answer them?

Read verses 20-30. Why did they not seize Him? What did Jesus say that caused the Jews to question what He said?

What did Jesus tell them in verse 24? What did He challenge them to do?

In verse 25, what question did they ask? In this confrontation, Jesus gives them a clear answer. Will anyone believe?

In verses 28-29, what did Jesus mean by "When you lift up the Son of Man"? Pay close attention to verse 29. What does it say about the Father? Will the Father ever leave Jesus? Why is this true? What does that say about your relationship to the Father?

Now read verses 31-51. Who was Jesus directly speaking to? What did He call for them to do and what did He promise in verses 31-32?

In verses 33-38, what was their reaction and how did Jesus answer them? Remember, at this time, the Romans had them in bondage. Why did Jesus address their slavery to sin instead?

In verses 39-47, who did Jesus say their Father is? How do we know if God is really someone's Father? What is the difference between those who hear and understand Jesus' words and those who do not?

Now we come to the climax where Jesus will announce who He is. Look at verses 48-59. What did they say to insult Jesus? How did Jesus respond and what does He promise if they will keep His words? What does it mean to keep His words?

What did Jesus say about Abraham? In verse 58, the English words, "I AM" in Hebrew would be YHWH or Jehovah. This is the very name of God given to us in Exodus 3:14. Knowing this, what was Jesus clearly saying about Himself? What were the reactions of these people who believed in Him at the beginning of His time of ministry?

Are there people today who only want to see Jesus as a teacher and not God? Will those people have a relationship with Him and see His promises at work in their lives?

What did you learn about Jesus today?

Write a prayer praising Jesus for who you know Him to be. Commit to be a person who continues in His Word and keeps His Word. Ask Him to help you get to know Him more.

DAY 53

Jesus Journeys To Jerusalem

John the Apostle gave seven signs that would prove Jesus to be the Messiah. We now come to the sixth of those signs. Jesus is still in Jerusalem and it is now the Sabbath.

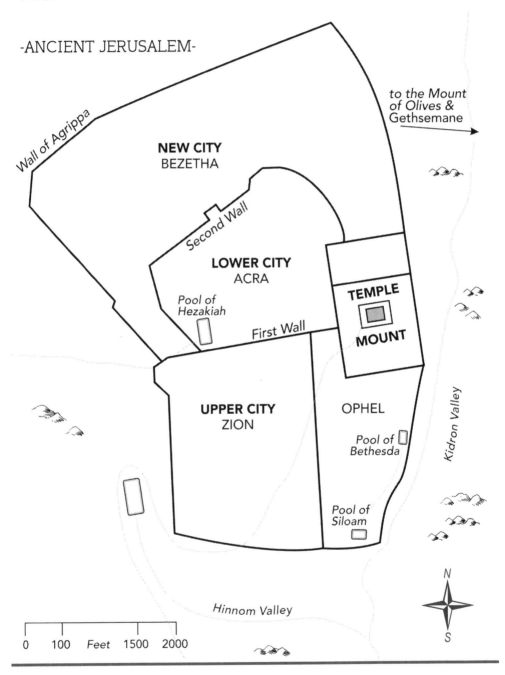

-ANCIENT JERUSALEM-

Read John 9:1-41.

Looking at verses 1-5, what question did the Disciples ask? What assumption did they make when they saw someone in a state of suffering? Do people make this same assumption today?

What was Jesus' answer to their question? When something bad happens to you, how would this truth apply? How does Jesus' statement about Himself apply to their question and to us when we are in a bad situation?

What did Jesus do in verses 6-16? What did He tell the man to do? What was the result? Knowing it was the Sabbath, why would this be a problem for some?

Looking at verses 17-23, what did the blind man say about Jesus? What was the answer his parents gave and why did they give it?

Read verses 24-25 again. What did the blind man assert about Jesus? Could you say the same about who Jesus is and what He has done for you? What does true life transformation tell others about Jesus?

Look again at the exchange between the blind man and the Pharisees in verses 26-34. What did the man who was healed by Jesus say about Him? What was the result of his brave rebuttal?

In verses 35-41, we find a very touching and revealing moment with Jesus and the man He healed. What did Jesus ask the man and how did he answer? How powerful is the statement "you have seen him," knowing this man had been blind all his life?

What is the man's reaction to Jesus' revelation as the Son of Man, the Messiah? He worshipped Jesus and He does not stop him. Why is this significant?

What stands out most to you from this day in Jesus' life? What did you learn about Him?

Write a prayer asking Jesus to open your eyes to see what you are supposed to see and to show you things He wants you to know. Ask Him to open the eyes of people you know who are blind to who He is. Pray He will give you an opportunity to share with them all that Jesus has done in your life.

DAY 54
Jesus Journeys To Jerusalem

Jesus is still in Jerusalem and He has caused a stir. He forgave the woman caught in adultery and healed a man who was blind from birth. He clearly stated to the crowd He was, and is, God. Now, He illustrates the relationship we are to have with Him as our Good Shepherd.

Psalm 23 is a cherished section of scripture with a promise of who God is to us and how He will take care of us. As Jesus taught, this Psalm must have been brought to mind.

Read John 10:1-21.
According to verses 1-5, how do the sheep know the Shepherd from the thief? Do you feel you know the voice of the Lord?

Now look at verses 6-10. What does Jesus promise if we will come to Him to be His? What would it mean to a sheep for it to go in and go out and find pasture? How would that apply to your life?

What is the difference between the thief and Jesus as our Shepherd? What does it mean to have life, and life abundantly? Are you experiencing the abundant life? If so, what is happening? If not, why?

What does the good Shepherd do? Did Jesus do that for you? What does it mean to you that He would do that for you?

What does Jesus tell us in verses 14-16? How does this apply to you? What is this saying about the relationship we are to have with Jesus?

What does Jesus reveal to us in verses 17-18? What do you learn about Jesus in these verses?

How did people react to Jesus and what He taught, in verses 19-21?

Read John 10:22-42.
The Feast of the Dedication is Hanukkah. Jesus celebrated Hanukkah. This is the Feast of the Lights which commemorated the re-consecration of the Temple by Judas Maccabeus in 165 BC. This was the last great deliverance God had given to the Jewish people.

Two months have passed since Jesus' last confrontation with the Jews.

What did they ask of Him in verse 24?

What did Jesus say to them in verses 25-30? Why did He say they do not understand what He has been telling them? What did He say about His sheep? What did He say about Himself in verse 30? Do you feel that His message is clear?

In verses 31-38, how did they react to what Jesus told them? Does Jesus seem afraid to you? What does this tell you about Him? What did Jesus say should have convinced them that He was telling the truth?

Now look at verses 39-42. What happened when they tried to seize Him? Where did Jesus go? Why do you think He traveled all that way? What effect did He have on many who heard Him and came to Him?

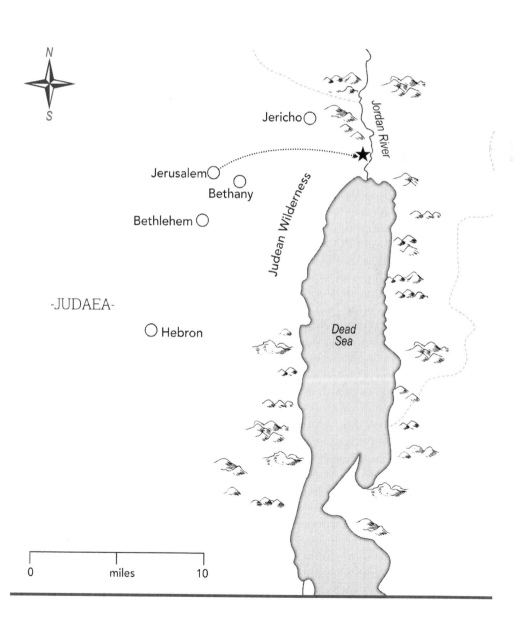

Write a prayer telling Jesus you want Him as your shepherd. Tell Him you want to be one who experiences the abundant life. Ask Him to show you any area the "thief" is seeking to steal or destroy. Pray for others who are in the clutches of the "thief."

DAY 55
Jesus Journeys To Jerusalem

After the violent confrontations Jesus experienced in Jerusalem, He journeyed to the place His public ministry started, Galilee. There, many came to Him and became believers. This would be His last time to come home. After this short stay, He would make his final journey to Jerusalem where He would be arrested, tortured and crucified.

Read Luke 10:1-24

What did Jesus do in Luke 10:1-3? How is this different than what He did before? Why did He choose to do this now?

What instructions did He give to them in verses 4-11?

According to verses 17-24, what were the results of the mission of the seventy? What did Jesus tell them was happening and what did He say He had given them? What are they to rejoice in? What causes Jesus joy?

Write a prayer asking to be a laborer in the Harvest. Ask Him to bring to mind people you should be praying for and sharing with. Ask Him to give you victory over the enemy. Tell Him your joy is not in what you have, but in that He has you.

DAY 56

Jesus now begins His journey toward Jerusalem. He has an appointment with the Cross that He cannot be late for. To the Apostles, the Samaritans are not showing Jesus the respect He deserves. What they do not know is that God is in the details.

Luke 9:51-62.
Focusing on Luke 9:51-56, what will soon happen to Jesus? Where must this take place? What was Jesus' attitude about this?

Why did the Samaritans not receive Jesus and His Disciples? Have there been times in your life when something seemed to get in the way of what you wanted to do or where you wanted to go? Has it ever turned out that God was behind it all?

What was James and John's reaction when they were not welcomed? Do you see why they were called the "Sons of Thunder"? Was this a sign of their old nature coming out? What did James and John not know? What did Jesus share with them?

As Christians, should we check our frustration and anger, trusting that God has us? Is it possible that God wants us to be somewhere else, at a different time, than we had planned? Have you seen God work this way for His purpose in your life?

Look at verses 57-62. When the man said he would follow Jesus, Jesus warned him that if he does, life would not be easy. Jesus would know; He is on His way to be killed in only a few days.

What did Jesus say to the other two who were called to follow Him? What is this telling you about the priority Jesus must have in your relationships and life? Are you willing to follow him completely with no looking back?

Write a prayer asking Jesus to reveal a time that He frustrated your plans to fulfill His purpose. Tell Him you will trust Him in every circumstance and you will look for Him when things are not going your way.

▬ LIFE GROUP DISCUSSION QUESTIONS ◼

DISCUSS THESE QUESTIONS TOGETHER:

1. In Day 49 of the journal, we were reminded that restoration and redemption is always the goal. Matthew 18:15-20 gives us a guide to live by when we're at odds with someone. What are you to do first? How can social media hinder this from happening? What can you do to ensure that you are living according to the Word in this way, and not according to the world?

2. Read John 8:6-9. What words do you think Jesus was writing on the ground? What do you need Jesus to meet you on the ground about?

3. When the disciples saw someone in a state of suffering, they jumped to a conclusion. What was that conclusion? Read John 9:1-5 to find out. Have you ever caught yourself falling into the same line of thinking?

4. What do you credit as a consequence of sin rather than an opportunity for Christ's power to be made known? We can find proper perspective in John 9:3.

5. The blind man's parents, in John 9:17-23, allowed someone else to speak for them. When given the opportunity to share about Christ and His power, they allowed someone else to speak out of fear for what consequences may come. Have you ever let someone else speak of Christ's power in fear of what may happen if you share the gospel?

►LIFE GROUP DISCUSSION QUESTIONS◄

APPLY WHAT YOU'VE LEARNED THIS
WEEK BY PUTTING IT INTO PRACTICE:

LOVE LIKE JESUS

In John 8, we read about a woman who was caught in the act of adultery. She was brought out before many, including Christ, to be put to death. According to the law of the time, both she and the man caught in the act with were to be put to death, but she was the only one brought forward. Jesus' response was not to have the man brought forward and both put to death. Instead He chooses grace and love. 1 Peter 4:8 reminds us that love covers a multitude of sins. This week, when you are tempted to call out someone's sin, choose to extend love and grace instead.

INTENTIONAL INTIMACY

Read John 10:1-21. Do you know when you are hearing the voice of God? The more time we spend with Him and in His Word, the better understanding we will have of who He is and what His voice sounds like. If you aren't currently spending time with the Lord daily, start today!

FULLY SURRENDERED

What does it mean to have "life abundantly?" Are you experiencing the abundant life? Why or why not? If not, have you fully surrendered your time, talent, and treasure to Him?

EXPERIENCE MORE

How can we show the forgiveness of Jesus Christ in our community?

DAY 57
Jesus Journeys Toward Jerusalem

Jesus and His Disciples are getting close to Bethany, which is home to Lazarus, Martha and Mary.

After the encounter with the Samaritans, Jesus had an opportunity to teach His Disciples a vital lesson, when a lawyer approached, testing Him.

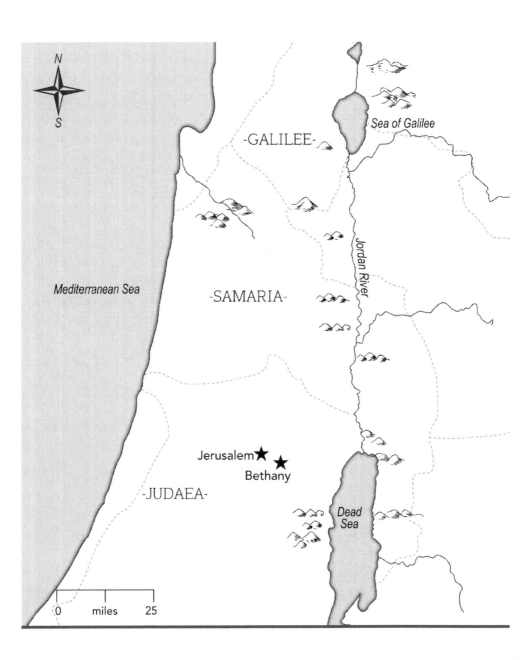

Read Luke 10:25-29.
What question did the lawyer ask Jesus? What question did Jesus ask in return?
What correct answer did the attorney give?

What did the lawyer ask, in hopes of justifying himself?

Read Jesus' response in Luke 10:30-37.
Remember that Samaritans were considered to be vile and accursed people. The division between them and the Jews was to the point of hatred. Are there groups today that feel this way about each other? Does this parable apply to them?

Which two people will not help the man in trouble? Who, in modern day, would be like these two people? What does that tell you about righteousness not being a title or position but a practice?

What did the Samaritan do to help the man? Was there a cost to his compassion?

Who is your neighbor and how does this apply to your life?

Write a prayer asking God to give you a heart to love all the people He has placed around you. Ask Him to give you eyes to see the needs that you have been chosen to meet. Ask Him to show you ways you can love and make a real difference.

DAY 58

Jesus and the Disciples have arrived at Bethany and are in the home of Lazarus, Martha and Mary. It was the custom of the day to serve a meal when someone came into your home. Middle Eastern meals were true feasts. In fact, they had a pre-meal that consisted of more food than most of us would eat today. Then there is the main meal, followed by dessert. Martha was tasked with serving at least 16 people, most of whom were men who would eat a lot. To add to this stress, the guest of honor is Jesus!

Read Luke 10:38-42.
What was Martha trying to do and where was Mary? Where did Martha think that Mary should be? Can you relate to how Martha felt?

What question did Martha ask Jesus? Does this remind you of the question the Apostles asked when they were in the storm and thought they would perish (Mark 4:38)? Are you ever left wondering if the Lord cares?

How did Jesus describe Martha's condition? What caused her to feel this way?

What did Jesus say about Mary? What was the one necessary thing? Are you more of a Martha or a Mary? Have you chosen the one necessary thing? If you do, what does Jesus promise you?

Write a prayer asking God to give you a mind filled with peace, not worry. Tell Him what you do worry about and ask Him to take the worry away. Commit to being more like Mary, spending quality time with Him, listening to Him and learning from Him.

DAY 59

Jesus now makes a turn that must not have made sense to the Disciples. They were right next to Jerusalem and yet, Jesus turned to go back to the Judean wilderness. They must have wondered why. They would soon know.

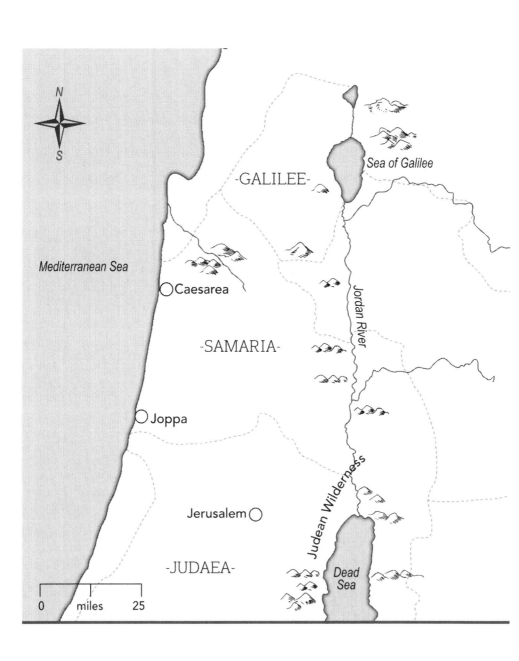

Read Luke 11:1-13.
What did Jesus do and what did it cause the Disciples to ask? What had John taught his disciples?

What did Jesus teach them in verses 2-4? Remember that He also taught this in the Sermon on the Mount. Why did He bring them back to it again? What does that tell you about His leadership? What stands out to you in the Lord's Prayer?

Focus on verses 5-8. What is Jesus teaching us about effective prayer? What does it mean to pray with persistence? What are you to do until you get an answer?

Now look at verses 9-10. What does this teach us about how passionate our prayers should be? How is knocking and seeking, a sign of persistence? What does Jesus promise if we pray this way? Is this how you pray?

Look at verses 11-13. What point is Jesus making? Will God, being a good Father, give us something that is bad for us even though we ask for it? Why or why not?

What does Jesus say about the Holy Spirit? Even though Christians are given the gift of the Holy Spirit, do you see that we are to ask for fillings of the Holy Spirit?

Write a list of things that you are praying God will do for you. What needs are you hoping He will meet? What blessings do you desire? Who do you want to know the Lord? What relationships do you want Him to give to you? Pray through these passionately. Commit to being persistent in your prayers until the He answers you. Then, ask for Him to fill you with the Holy Spirit.

➤➤➤NOTES➤

DAY 60
Jesus Travels To The Judean Wilderness

Jesus had been performing the most incredible miracles. There was no denying that He was able to do extraordinary things that no one had ever done before. When the Pharisees asked for a sign to prove He was from God, Jesus gave them exactly what they asked for. So, they were faced with a choice, either Jesus was from God or there was another explanation.

Read Luke 11:14-28 and Matthew 12:22-24. What were the crowds saying about Jesus? How did the Pharisees answer them? What did they attribute Jesus' miraculous powers to? Did they deny the miracles?

Now read Matthew 12:25-29. What did Jesus tell the Pharisees? What did He say about division in the Church? What about division in your family? What is Jesus saying in verse 28?

Focus on Matthew 12:30-32. What is Jesus telling us about being with Him or against Him? If someone is not with Him, then what does that mean?

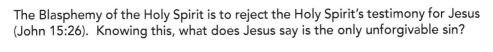

The Blasphemy of the Holy Spirit is to reject the Holy Spirit's testimony for Jesus (John 15:26). Knowing this, what does Jesus say is the only unforgivable sin?

Now, read verses 33-37. What does Jesus say to do? What is the choice we need to make?

According to verses 35-37, where do our words come from? What does the things we say reveal about us? What will we all be held accountable for on the judgment day?

Write a prayer asking God to give you a heart to believe in Him. Pray for those who have been indifferent or cold toward Jesus. Pray for unity in your Church, family, place of work, anywhere you have relationships. Think about the way you speak and the words you use. Pray, asking Him to show you what is truly in your heart.

DAY 61
Jesus Travels To The Judean Wilderness

Jesus is still engaged with the Pharisees. They watched Him heal a man and there was no denying the man was healed. Now they ask for something truly shocking, regardless of His miracles.

Read Matthew 12:38-45
What did the Pharisees ask for in verse 38? How many miracles had they already seen? What did Jesus say was the ultimate sign that they still would not believe?

Who did Jesus say will rise up at the judgment and testify against the Pharisees?

The men of Nineveh repented at the preaching of Jonah. The Queen of the South traveled the world to hear the Wisdom of Solomon. What does this say about our passion to learn from Jesus who is even greater than our most admired teachers?

What warning did Jesus give in verses 43-45? Does this shed light on how a man could have 6,000 demons?

Write a prayer asking God to keep your heart open to the Holy Spirit's testimony of Jesus. Pray for people you know who need to be moved to Him and by Him.

DAY 62
Jesus Travels To The Judean Wilderness

Jesus was kind, but truthful. He did not draw back when it was time to stand-up against injustice. Pay attention to the words Jesus used when He confronted the Pharisees. Don't miss the tension that would have risen to an intolerable level.

Read Luke 37-54. Where was Jesus when this confrontation occurred? Why did He not ceremonially wash His hands? What does this tell you about Him?

Look at verses 37-41. What did Jesus tell them? What does this tell you about what God values? What does this mean God wants to be true of you? How could you do this?

Read verse 42 along with Matthew 23:23. What are the weightier, most important aspects of the Law? According to Jesus, was tithing one of the least of the commands? Did He tell them that they should tithe? What else did He tell them to do?

Look at verses 43-44. What did Jesus say they were doing wrong? How important are our motives to God? Can anything be hidden from God?

The Lawyers realized Jesus was making a case against them, too. What did the Lawyer say to Jesus and how did Jesus respond in verses 45-52? Write down what He said they were doing that would render a guilty verdict against them. Write down what He said they would do one day. How do you think the Apostles felt when they heard Jesus say what would be done to them?

Why was it time for Jesus to deal so boldly and bluntly with the Pharisees and Lawyers?

What does this interaction tell you about Jesus? Was He strong or was He weak? Was He afraid to address an issue? Did He do it clearly?

Write a prayer asking the Lord to show where you are hiding your true motives and your true self. Ask Him to give you the wisdom to live a life of integrity. Ask Him to show you how to willingly face issues with kindness, to bring about the truth.

DAY 63
Jesus Travels To The Judean Wilderness

Jesus went straight from the conflict with the Pharisees and Lawyers to send a critical message to the crowd that had gathered. He explained that religious hypocrisy is an insidious evil that turns people from God and then condemns them to hell.

Read Luke 12:1-54.
What warning did Jesus give in verses 1-3? Why would the Apostles need to be on guard concerning this? Do you feel you and your church should be aware of shifting from a true relationship with God to a religious show?

What does Jesus say about our private thoughts, words and actions?

In verses 4-7, what and who does Jesus say we should fear? Remember, the Pharisees were willing to go to great lengths in order to silence anyone in opposition to them. Look back at Luke 11:49. How does his message relate to the message He gives now? Why is it important to know they are precious to God? Why is it important for you to have a balance between fearing the Lord and knowing how much He loves you?

In verses 8-12, what did Jesus say about the need to share our love for Him without fear or shame? What happens if we do not? Why is the blasphemy of the Spirit taught here? What did Jesus tell them to trust in if they are ever put on the spot? What does this mean to you about how you should live and how you should share your faith?

In verses 13-15, a man interrupts Jesus with a selfish request. How did Jesus answer and what does He warn us about? Do you believe what Jesus said?

Jesus tells a parable in verses 16-21. What is the message of the parable? What made the man foolish and why? Do you understand why he was condemned to hell?

What should the rich man have done? What does his view of money say about his heart? Are you rich in God or do you see all your money as your own?

Read verses 22-32. What is Jesus telling us not to do? How does knowing that God cares for you accomplish this? In verse 31, what are we told to seek after? What will happen when we do?

What does Jesus tell us to do in verses 33-34? Note that He does not say to sell all your possessions but to sell some. Do you have things you could sell to aid the poor?

Look at verses 35-40. How does Jesus want us to live? How important is this, knowing how close the time of His second coming is? What should we be doing? What should you be doing? What does He promise if you are faithful?

Look at Peter's question in verse 41 and how Jesus answers him in verses 42-48. Who was Jesus talking to? What is He saying we should do? What does He say about how judgment will be given out? Who is treated more severely? Do you know what God's will is for you?

Focus on verses 49-53. What did Jesus say He came to do? Did most people understand this about Him? What did Jesus say He must undergo and how did He feel knowing it was coming?

Why will people be divided over who Jesus is and what He calls for us to do? Have you experienced this and with who?

Jesus brought this time of teaching to a powerful conclusion in verses 54-59. What does He tell us regarding the signs of the times? Why does He tell us to live just lives?

What did you learn about Jesus today? Of what you studied, what stands out most?

Write a prayer sharing your feelings with God. Tell Him what concerns you and that you trust He will take care of you. Ask Him for the wisdom to mend unhealthy relationships. Ask Him to give you boldness to speak out for Jesus.

►LIFE GROUP DISCUSSION QUESTIONS◄

DISCUSS THESE QUESTIONS TOGETHER:

1. When the world around us seems to be falling apart, what reason do we have to rejoice? Read Luke 10:17-24.

2. Do you have a difficult time letting go of frustrations when you find yourself somewhere other than where you had envisioned or planned? Have you experienced a time where being somewhere different than where you desired allowed God to fulfill a greater purpose in your life? Look at Luke 9:57-62. Do you think Jesus would have rather been somewhere other than on the way to His death?

3. What must we do to inherit the kingdom of God? Read Luke 10:27-28.

4. Division and hatred are not a new phenomenon. In Luke 10:30-37, we see Jesus' response to such behavior. How have you participated in such behavior towards another group of people? What role have you played in the past? What role does Christ call you to now?

►LIFE GROUP DISCUSSION QUESTIONS◄

APPLY WHAT YOU'VE LEARNED THIS
WEEK BY PUTTING IT INTO PRACTICE:

LOVE LIKE JESUS

As you walked with Jesus this past week, what has Jesus said about your fears?

INTENTIONAL INTIMACY

Over the course of the week, revisit the things you have been asking of the Lord. Tell Him the desires of your heart and commit to persistently praying for such things.

FULLY SURRENDERED

Is Jesus the number one priority in your life? Do you have relationships that come before Him? Luke 9:59-62 makes the position and priority of Christ in our lives clear.

EXPERIENCE MORE

If you could choose one place in all the world to travel to while telling others about Jesus, where would you go?

DAY 64
Jesus Travels To The Judean Wilderness

On the same day Jesus had been teaching, He is told that Pilate had killed some Galileans. It is almost certain that Jesus knew these men. The question that leads into the next subject He addresses is 'do bad things only happen to bad people?'

Read Luke 13:1-9.
What was Jesus told in verses 1-6? What does Jesus tell us about tragedy and the people it happens to? What does He say about the 'fairness' of life? What should we know and do based on this?

How does the parable in verses 6-9 relate to what Jesus just said? What does this say about people who do not live their lives with purpose and meaning? While God is patient, does their come a point when He will no longer wait for you to do what you are supposed to be doing? Does the farmer do everything possible to give the tree a chance to produce fruit? Has God given you every opportunity to do what you are supposed to do with your life?

After Jesus addressed the crowd, He went to the Synagogue to continue teaching. There was a woman there who needed His touch. She was one of the reasons He made this final excursion into the Judean area before going to Jerusalem to die.

Read verses 10-17.
What was the woman's condition? What did Jesus do for her and what was her reaction? How do you think she felt?

What was the reaction of the Synagogue official? What was Jesus' response to him? What did Jesus say about the woman and how much she mattered to God? What does Jesus say about his opponent's priorities? People relied on oxen and donkeys to earn a living. So, how would caring for their animals reveal their values? What was the result of Jesus putting them in their place?

What have you learned about Jesus in this section? What kind of a person was He?

Write a prayer asking the Lord to show you how to love and care for those in need. Ask Him to guide you in making people a priority over things. Ask Him to show you your purpose and the fruit you should bear.

DAY 65

Jesus now moves to the city of Jericho. There were two men He wanted to touch there before going to the Cross. One was a blind man named Bartimaeus (Mark 10:46) and the other was a Tax Collector named Zaccheus. They both go above and beyond to see Jesus.

Read Luke 18:35-43.
In verses 35-39, how much passion did Bartimaeus show when he realized Jesus was near? Why did people tell him to be quiet? What did he do in response?

What did Jesus ask him in verses 40-43? What did Jesus then do for him? What was the result?

Jesus now enters the city of Jericho. Read 19:1-10.
What are we told about Zaccheus in verses 1-3?

Look at verse 4. How badly did he want to see Jesus? What did Zaccheus have in common with Bartimaeus and the woman who had a hemorrhage for 12 years? What does this tell you about the need to be passionate and persistent when you pray?

What did Jesus say to Zaccheus in verses 5-6? What was his reaction? Why is it significant that Jesus would go to his house and eat with him? What does this tell you about Jesus?

Now read verses 7-10. How did the people react when Jesus went to spend time with Zaccheus? What did Jesus say was His purpose, in verse 10? Is this your purpose and the purpose of your Church?

Look at verse 8. What effect did Jesus' love have on Zaccheus? How serious was Zaccheus about repenting? How important is it that we have the fruit of repentance?

Write a prayer naming the lost people you know and pray passionately the Lord will bring them to repentance. Pray that you will be a person who seeks, and is used, to save the lost. Pray your Church will be a place where sinners are welcome and the lost are found.

DAY 66

The seventh sign John gave proving Jesus as the Messiah was the raising of Lazarus.

Jesus is in the Judean wilderness and receives word that Lazarus is sick. He is approximately 21 miles away from Bethany, where Lazarus is. Once Jesus arrives in Bethany, He will be on the door step of Jerusalem and his date with the Cross.

Read John 11.
Look at verses 1-6. How did Jesus feel about Lazarus? What did Jesus do when He heard He was sick? Why did He do this? Have you had a time when you wanted Jesus to act quickly and He did not? Why do think Jesus waited to intercede?

How did the Disciples respond, in verses 7-10, when Jesus announced they would return to Bethany? Did it make sense to them to go back to the area of Jerusalem? What did Jesus tell them? 'Walking in the light' means that we live in the will of God. How does this apply to what Jesus told them?

Looking at verses 10-16, what did Jesus tell them about Lazarus? How badly did the Disciples not want to return to Jerusalem? When Jesus said Lazarus was dead and He was glad, what did He mean? What did Jesus want to happen in them because of this?

What did Thomas say? How committed was he to Jesus?

According to verses 17-22, what happened when Jesus arrived in Bethany?
What did Martha say to Him and what did she believe about Him?

Look at verses 23-27. What did Jesus say about Himself? What does He promise
if you believe in Him? Do you believe it? What did Martha declare regarding
what she believes about Him?

In verses 28-37, we see the love Jesus has for Mary and how much He cares
when we are hurting. What did Mary say to Jesus? What are we told about
Jesus and how He was feeling in verse 33? What does this tell you about Jesus?
Do you believe Jesus feels this deeply for you?

Look at verse 35 again. What did Jesus do? He knew He would raise Lazarus, so why did He weep? What does this say about how Jesus feels with us, as well as for us?

The great sign takes place in verses 38-44. What did Jesus say would happen if Mary believes? Is that promise for us, too? What did Jesus say about His relationship with the Father?

Jesus could have removed the stone and unwrapped Lazarus himself, yet He told others to do it. He was the only one who could raise Lazarus from the dead. What does that tell you about how Jesus works with us? How does He want to work with you? What are you told to do? What will He do that only He can do?

Now read verses 45-57.
What were the different reactions to the seventh sign?

What did Caiaphas say about Jesus? Look carefully at verse 51. God spoke through a man who did not believe in Jesus. Did you know that God speaks through people? Has someone ever said something to you and you knew the message was from God? Could you be more attentive, knowing God may use others to speak to you?

Write a prayer asking the Lord to make you aware of what He wants you to do, asking Him to do only what He can do. Ask for Him to move in a way that you cannot miss. Pray that you will hear and listen when He is speaking to you.

DAY 67

Jesus is now traveling to Jerusalem for the final time to bring fulfillment to His purpose. This was the "must" of His life. He had spent three years preparing for this moment. He would be betrayed, arrested, tortured, crucified and would rise from the dead; everything He taught would be met. He would take on the sins of the world so that we could be forgiven if we would believe in Him.

Read Luke 13:22-35.
What question was Jesus asked in verse 23? How did He answer? How does His answer differ from what most people believe? Look at Matthew 7:13-14 and note that Jesus had taught this before.

According to verse 29, while only a few are saved, where do they come from? Look at Isaiah 25:6-9. What does this tell you the feast in the Kingdom of God will be like?

Look at Luke 13:31-33. What did the Pharisees say to Jesus and what was His response? What was the goal that Jesus referred to? How purposeful is Jesus? What does this tell you about Him?

Look at verses 34-35. What did Jesus say concerning Jerusalem? What did He want to do for them? Why would it not happen? Were they given a choice? Does Jesus want to reach everyone with His love? Why do some receive the life He has for them and others do not?

Write a prayer thanking the Lord for giving people a choice. Thank Him for not forcing this life on anyone; we can choose to love Him if we want to. Pray for those who you know that have not chosen to love Jesus. Ask that their eyes and hearts may be opened to Him.

DAY 68
Jesus' Journey To Jerusalem And The Cross

Jesus did not have much time left with the Disciples. He was not only preparing them for His death, He was equipping them to take on a mission. He would successfully accomplish His purpose and He wanted them to do the same. So, He teaches them what may at first be a shocking lesson.

Read Luke 16:1-9.
What did the manager do when he realized he was about to be fired? What was the master's response when he discovered what he did? What lesson does Jesus want us to learn?

What does Jesus tell us about using material things for Spiritual purposes? Why would the Apostles need to know this? Why would you need to know this? Are you doing this?

Look at Luke 16:10-13. What does Jesus say about faithfulness? Are you faithful with the wealth Jesus has allowed you to have? In reality, is the money you have yours or is it money God has entrusted you with?

How many masters can someone truly serve? Why does Jesus warn us we cannot serve Him and money?

According to Matthew 23:23, Jesus tells us that tithing is the least of the commands. Are you faithful in this area? If someone is not faithful in this area, are they faithful in the more important things? If God cannot trust someone to tithe, will He entrust them with more?

Read Luke 16:14-18.
What was the reaction of the Pharisees when they heard what Jesus taught? Why did they react this way? Do people today react this way to God's teaching on money?

How did Jesus respond to them? What does Jesus say about our hearts? What does Jesus say about the Word of God?

The Pharisees taught and practiced that divorce was okay. What did Jesus say about this? Why did He bring this up now?

Now look at Luke 16:19-30.
What is Jesus teaching in this parable? Why is He teaching this now? What is He telling the Pharisees? What does this tell you about eternal punishment and eternal life?

Write a prayer and commit to the Lord that you will be faithful in the area of money. Ask Jesus to give you the wisdom to use all He has given you for His purposes. Pray that He can entrust the true riches to you. Pray that He will use you in amazing ways.

DAY 69

Jesus knew the agony that He would soon be facing. He was aware of the tortuous pain that would be inflicted on Him. Soon the sins of the world would be laid upon His body and they would tear His heart. Only one person was sensitive to how He felt and she did something extravagant to show Him love and care.

Read John 12:1-11.
Look at verses 1-3. What was Martha doing? What was Lazarus doing? What did Mary do?

There was a Jewish proverb at that time which said, "As an expensive fragrance will fill the house, so a good name will go throughout the world." How did Mary prophesy the name of Jesus?

Focus on verses 4-5.
What was Judas' reaction to Mary? What did he say should have been done with the money?

The perfume was worth a year's wages, so around $75,000 in our economy. Was Judas to say that it would have been better to give it to the poor than waste it showing love to Jesus? Are there people today making the same accusation against the Church when we show how much we love Jesus in an extravagant way?

What was the real reason Judas attacked Mary?

What was Jesus' response to Judas? What did He say about Mary's actions? What did it mean to Jesus? What do you learn about Jesus from this?

Are you sensitive to the Lord's feelings? Do you think about how He feels when we worship Him? Do you think about how He feels when people are hurting? Do you know what gives Him joy? Do you know what angers Him? Do you know what grieves His Spirit?

Write a prayer thanking Jesus for enduring the pain of the cross for you. Ask Him to show you what makes Him joyous. Ask Him what you can do to show love and care for Him.

DAY 70

Jesus arrives at Jerusalem for the last time. This is an important day for the Jewish people and for the whole world. God told them the Messiah would come on this date and Jesus fulfilled that promise. Daniel wanted to learn about this timing, so God sent Gabriel to give him the answer. In Daniel 9:24-27, Daniel was told that 69 seven-year periods, or 482 years, would pass from the time a decree was given to restore and rebuild Jerusalem until the Messiah came. The decree was given on March 5th 444 BC. It is now March 30th 33 AD, the day Daniel was told the Messiah would come and then be killed as a sacrifice for others.

Read Luke 19:28-44 and Zechariah 9:9, a prophecy of the coming Messiah. What does it say about Him and what He will be like?

Look at Luke 29-38. What did Jesus have His Disciples do? How does this go with the prophecy Zechariah gave? What happened when Jesus came close to Jerusalem?

Look at verses 39-40. What was the reaction of the Pharisees? How did Jesus respond? The Pharisees knew the prophecies of Daniel and Zechariah concerning the Messiah. How could they not have realized who Jesus was?

Focus on verses 41-44. How did Jesus feel when He looked down on Jerusalem? What does this tell you about Him?

What did Jesus say would happen to Jerusalem? Why did He say this would occur?

God had offered the children of Israel a choice between being blessed and being cursed. He wanted to love and bless them; they chose the curse because they did not recognize their "day," the day the Messiah came to them. In 70 AD, the Roman General Titus laid siege to Jerusalem and brought about a fulfillment of the curses found in Deuteronomy 28:47-57.

Read Deuteronomy 28:47-57 and write down what God said would occur. Be sure to take note that the eagle was the sign of the Roman Empire.

Looking back at what you just read, did God want this to happen to the Israelites? Did Jesus? Why did it happen? Are there people today who are living cursed lives and refuse to turn to God for help?

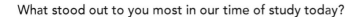

What stood out to you most in our time of study today?

Write a prayer committing to serve the Lord with joy and a glad heart. Tell Him that you want the blessed life He has planned for you. Ask God to make you aware of the signs of our time. Pray for people you know who need to turn to Jesus for His love and care.

►LIFE GROUP DISCUSSION QUESTIONS ◄

DISCUSS THESE QUESTIONS TOGETHER:

1. Many situations can cause us to utter the phrase "that's not fair." Read Luke 13:1-9 to see what Jesus tells us about tragedy and fairness. Are Christians exempt from such events and feelings? How does that impact your walk with the Lord? How do you share that with others who are curious about the Christian faith or new in their walk with Christ?

2. We were all created on purpose, for a purpose. Jesus shared His purpose in Luke 19:7-10. What was His purpose? What is our purpose? If we are the Church, where and with whom should our time be spent? How can you personally live this out?

3. Day 66 of the journal took us through John 11 and the story of Lazarus. Many people might overlook this story, since it's difficult to apply when you have not been raised from the dead. Jesus intentionally waited to heal Lazarus. Why did He wait? What has Jesus waited to do for you? At any point in the waiting, did your attitude change to a "why bother" when you didn't get what you had asked for? What happened when Jesus answered your prayers and gave you what you had been asking for?

4. Over and over in scripture we are told, "the gate is narrow." Read Matthew 7:13-14 and Luke 13:22-35 to see why Jesus consistently taught on this. Knowing that, do you frequently share this with other brothers and sisters in Christ as a reminder, or do you shy away because it's scary, harsh or even untrue?

5. "As an expensive fragrance will fill the house, so a good name will go throughout the world." We read this proverb in Day 69 of the journal. How did Mary's actions at the foot of Jesus foreshadow what would become of His name? What can you do to make your name a pleasant aroma for Christ?

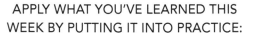
APPLY WHAT YOU'VE LEARNED THIS
WEEK BY PUTTING IT INTO PRACTICE:

LOVE LIKE JESUS
Refer to the list of names you wrote from Day 65 of the journal. As you are praying for each lost person by name, reach out to them and extend the love of Christ through an act of kindness or an invitation to join you for a service or LIFE Group.

INTENTIONAL INTIMACY
Persistence and passion are key to our prayers. In Luke 19:4, we see yet another case for such components being at the center of our prayer life. This week, be persistent and passionate as you come before the Lord with your prayers.

FULLY SURRENDERED
Prior to your time in the journal this week, did you know what spiritual purposes our material possessions are to be used for? Is this something that you currently follow? How can you improve on doing so? Remember, money is not ours, but Christ's. Our tithes are the least of the commands He has given us to show how faithful we will be in bigger areas.

EXPERIENCE MORE
If you didn't have barriers, what extravagant thing could you do to worship God?

DAY 71
Jesus Enters Jerusalem

When Jesus enters Jerusalem He goes to the Temple to find the money changers have returned. Again, He drives them out and cleanses the Temple so that it will be the Temple it was meant to be.

Read Matthew 21:12-22.
In verses 12-13, what did Jesus do and why did He do it? Look at 1 Corinthians 6:19. The Temple God loves the most is you. Are you a House of Prayer or a Den of Thieves? Are you truly devoted to prayer? Are there things you are indulging in that God would want you to be cleansed from?

According to verse 14, what did Jesus do after He cleansed the Temple? Do you see the significance of cleansing the Temple before miracles would take place? Is that also true of you and your life?

Look at verses 15-16. What did the Pharisees see and hear? How did they respond? What did Jesus tell them?

Jesus now leaves the Temple and goes back to Bethany. Read verses 17-19. What did Jesus do to the fig tree and why? What is the lesson we are to learn from this?

What was the reaction of the Disciples according to verses 20-22? What did Jesus teach about faith and prayer? Do you believe Him? How does the cleansing of the Temple followed by miracles apply to this?

Write a prayer asking the Lord to show you what needs cleansing from your life. Ask Him what steps you need to take to make this happen. Pray that you will be a person of prayer and will see mountains move. Ask the Lord to move any mountain you have in your life.

DAY 72
Jesus Enters Jerusalem

The Pharisees wanted Jesus gone. They wanted to find a way to remove Him or destroy Him. Now they are trying to discredit Him and they plan their final assault. If they succeed, they will not have to deal with the reaction from the huge crowd that loved Him.

Read Luke 20.
Look back at verses 1-8. What did the Pharisees ask Jesus? Why did they ask this?

Jesus often answers a question with a question. How did He trap them with the question He asked? How do you think this made the Pharisees feel?

In verses 9-18, Jesus used a parable to expose the Pharisees. What part of the parable seemed to shock the Pharisees the most? Who was the vineyard given to? What was Jesus saying when He quoted Psalm 118:22 concerning the stone that the builders rejected?

Are there leaders in our country who are seeking to cast Jesus and His Word aside? Are we paying the price for this? When we remove God from society, we end up with a Godless society. When someone does not have God in their life, they have a Godless life. Do you see that happening today?

In verses 19-20, what was the reaction of the Pharisees and Scribes? How do you think their reaction showed that they understood, but did not want to admit it?

Read verses 21-26. Why did they ask this question? What were they hoping to do to Jesus by asking it? How did Jesus answer them? What does His answer mean to us?

Read verses 27-40. What does this tell you about the Sadducees? What did Jesus answer them? What does this tell you about what we will be like in Heaven?

Looking at verses 41-47, what did Jesus say that proved the Messiah is greater than David? How did Jesus warn the Scribes? Remember, Jesus cleansed the Temple of financial robbers who forced people to buy animals and exchange money only from them. Thinking about this, how does God feel about people who use Christianity to become rich?

What does this section reveal to you about Jesus?

Write a prayer asking that we, as a society, will come to know the importance of having Jesus at the center of our lives. Pray that we will not be a people who reject Jesus and then suffer the consequences of a Godless society.

DAY 73
Jesus Enters Jerusalem

The Temple in Jerusalem was breathtaking. Herod had remodeled it making it a wonder to behold architecturally. The stones were massive and were covered in gold. So, as Jesus and the Disciples walked the Temple Mount, they noticed the buildings and something else.

Read Matthew 24:1 and Luke 21:1-5. What did the Disciples notice? What caught Jesus' attention? What did Jesus say about what He saw?

What does this tell you about the woman's faith? How much did she love God? How much did she trust God? How did Jesus feel about her? What does this tell you about Jesus?

Read Matthew 24:1-3 and Luke 21:5-7. Remember that Jesus wept over the city of Jerusalem because of the destruction it would undergo. Knowing this was on His mind, what did He say would happen to the Temple?

When Jesus told of the destruction that would come, the Disciples assume it would be a sign of the end of time. So, they ask Jesus two questions: 1) When will these things take place (the Temple be destroyed)? 2) What will be the sign of your coming at the end of the age? The books of Matthew and Mark only answer the second question: what are the signs of the second coming? Luke gives the answer to both questions.

Go to Luke 21. In verses 8-11, Jesus starts with a list of the signs of the second coming. Then, note in Luke 21:12, Jesus shares "before all these things," meaning before the signs of his coming begins, everything described in verses 12-24 would be fulfilled, including the destruction of the Temple. Note in verse 24 Jesus tells us that the City of Jerusalem and Temple Mount would be in Gentile (non-Jewish) hands until the "Time of the Gentiles" is fulfilled. The ending of the Time of the Gentiles is the sign that says His coming will soon take place.

Now looking at Matthew 24:4-41, Luke 21:8-11 and verses 25-27, along with Mark 13:5-27. Write down, in order, the signs of His second coming.

Now focus on Luke 21:28-36. What does Jesus tell us to do?

Of what you learned in this study, what stands out the most?

Write a prayer asking Jesus to make you aware of the signs of His coming. Pray that you will be ready. Pray that you will not be involved in things you should not be. Ask Him to show you your purpose in these last days.

DAY 74
Jesus Enters Jerusalem

Jesus is coming to the last hours He will have with the Apostles. A lot will occur at the Last Supper. Be sure to take the time to fully understand what you need to learn from this. This is a night like no other.

Jesus knew the last night of His life was coming. Read Luke 21:37-38 to see how He prepared for what He would face. What did Jesus do in His last days? What did you learn about Jesus? How can you apply this in your own life?

Now read Luke 22:1-6. Write down the person who was mentioned in this verse and what they did.

Verse 7 tells us something very significant. What is it and why is it important for us to know this?

Read verses 8-13. What does Jesus want them to do? How does He answer their question? What does this tell you about Jesus?

Now look at John 13:1-3. What did Jesus know? How did Jesus feel about the Apostles?

One of the things Peter and John should have arranged for was to have someone wash the feet of each person who came. This was the job of the lowest slave. What did Jesus do in John 13:3-11? What did Peter say to Jesus? What was Jesus' response?

According to John 13:12-17, why did Jesus do this? What are we to learn from this? What brings the blessing to us?

In verses Luke 22:14-16, what does Jesus say He desires? Why does He want this so badly? What does this tell you about how valuable the Apostles were to Jesus? Do you think He feels this way about you? How should you feel about spending time with Him?

In the Passover meal, the food and the cups of wine were symbolic of the Israeli children who were in bondage for the Egyptians. Then, God set them free. In Luke 22:17-18, Jesus took the first cup of wine and explained why this meal was significant. What did He tell them?

In Luke 22:19, Jesus picked up the "Bread of Affliction," reminding us of the afflictions we have each experienced. What does Jesus say this bread now symbolizes? What did He say that He will take on for you and from you? Does this show you how much He loves you? Have you allowed Him to remove this from your life?

In Luke 22:20, Jesus picked up the "cup of Elijah" which was the last cup at the end of the meal. It most often would not be partaken of due to the symbolism of Elijah drinking it before the coming of the Messiah. What does it mean that Jesus took and gave them this cup? Look at Matthew 26:28, what did Jesus say this cup meant? How important is this to you? What does this say about His love for you?

Now look at Luke 22:21-24 and John 13:18-30. Jesus clearly said He would be betrayed and pointed out who would betray Him. Why did the Apostles miss that it was Judas? What were they arguing over that made them not get what Jesus was saying? Do you think there are times you get distracted by your self-interest and miss what matters most?

Did the Apostles understand the lesson taught when Jesus washed their feet? Why was this lesson so easy to forget? Do you forget to put others first?

Look at John 13:29-35. What does Jesus tell you about Himself? What command did He give us? What will happen when we take the command seriously and live out what He wants us to do? Are you obedient to this command? How can you follow-through?

What did Peter ask and how did Jesus respond in John 13:36-38?

Now look at Luke 22:31-34. What did Jesus tell Peter was happening in heaven at that very moment? What did Jesus say He was doing for Peter? What is Peter to do after he undergoes his trial? What does this tell you about how Jesus felt about Peter? What does this tell you about how Jesus feels about you, even when you fail?

In Luke 22:35-38, what did Jesus tell them is different now that He will be leaving them? What are they to do now? What does Jesus tell them about Himself?

Ask God to show you what He wanted you to learn in today's study and write it down. Write a prayer committing to put others first and to love people like Jesus loves them.

>>>—NOTES—→

DAY 75

As His betrayal approached, Jesus led the Apostles from the Upper Room to the Garden of Gethsemane.

Before they left the Upper Room, Jesus gave the teachings found in John 14-16 and prayed the prayer of John 17. After that, they went to the garden at the Mount of Olives.

Read Matthew 26:36-39. What did Matthew tell us happened? How was Jesus feeling? What did Jesus want the Disciples to do?

Read Luke 22:39-44. What did Jesus pray for? What was He committed to no matter what? Note that Luke is a Doctor. What did Luke say the stress did to Jesus physically? What does this tell you about Jesus?

When Jesus finished this first prayer, He returns to the Disciples. Look at Matthew 26:40-41. What were the Disciples doing? What did Jesus say to them? Did He condemn them or did He show understanding toward them? What does Jesus tell us about prayer and temptation?

Read Matthew 26:42-46. What did Jesus pray again and what was His commitment to the Father? Did Jesus demonstrate how we need to continue praying until we get an answer?

Now the time of His betrayal and arrest has come. Look at Luke 22:47-53. What did Judas do as he betrayed Jesus? How did Jesus respond to him?

Knowing what you just read, look at Matthew 26:51-56. What did Jesus do when Peter (see John 18:10) struck Malchus and cut off his ear? What did He tell them? What do we learn about Jesus taking the time to heal Malchus when He was facing such agony? What does this say to you about how we need to care for people who come against us?

Could Jesus have called for the Angels to intercede and stop this? Why did He not put an end to what was happening?

Jesus said to pray that we not enter into temptation. Write a prayer asking the Lord to show you areas where you need to flee from temptation. Ask Him to give you victory over sins in your life. Ask Him to reveal how you can show real love to people who are against you.

DAY 76
The Garden of Gethsemane

Jesus is now facing a mockery of a trial that will lead to the Cross. Remember, He has been up all night, praying intensely, so He must be extremely exhausted.

He had come for such a time as this. This was His purpose and even though He knew the pain that awaited Him, we are told "for the joy set before Him, He endured the cross despising the shame." (Hebrews 12:2). The joy was in forgiving the sins of those who believe in Him. The joy is knowing His love and the life that He has for us.

Read Matthew 26:57-67.
Jesus was brought to trial, first before Annas, and then before Caiaphas with the Sanhedrin. This consisted of 70 religious Leaders who ruled the Jewish nation. What were the Jewish leaders trying to do to Jesus? How did Jesus initially respond to them? When Jesus did answer, what did He say? Did He know what their reaction would be? How did they respond?

Read Luke 22:54-62. What did Peter do? How did Jesus respond and what was Peter's reaction? Would you have felt the same?

Read Luke 23:1-7. What did Pilate say concerning Jesus? What did they continue to say about Jesus? What does this tell you about the way Jesus taught?

Looking at Luke 23:8-12, what happened to Jesus when He came before Herod?

In Luke 23:13-25, we see Jesus brought back before Pilate. What does Pilate clearly state in verses 14-15? How could he later condemn Jesus to death knowing He is innocent?

Read Matthew 27:19-23. What did Pilate's wife report to him? What did she say about Jesus? How did she know this?

Read John 18:38. What did Jesus tell Pilate about Himself?

Crucifixion was a horrible and painful way to die, but they made it worse when they scourged Him and made Him carry the cross.

To understand what Jesus really went through, read the Medical explanation of what Jesus endured on the day He died, by Dr. C. Truman Davis.

Preparations for Jesus' scourging were carried out at Caesar's orders. The prisoner was stripped of His clothing and His hands tied to a post above His head. The Roman legionnaire stepped forward with the flagrum, or flagellum, in his hand. This was a short whip consisting of several heavy, leather thongs with two small balls of lead attached near the ends of each. The heavy whip was brought down with full force again and again across Jesus' shoulders, back, and legs. At first the weighted thongs cut through the skin only. Then, as the blows continued, they cut deeper into the subcutaneous tissues, producing first an oozing of blood from the capillaries and veins of the skin and finally spurting arterial bleeding from vessels in the underlying muscles.

The small balls of lead first produced large deep bruises that were broken open by subsequent blows. Finally, the skin of the back was hanging in long ribbons, and the entire area was an unrecognizable mass of torn, bleeding tissue. When it was determined by the centurion in charge that the prisoner was near death, the beating was finally stopped.

MOCKERY

The half-fainting Jesus was then untied and allowed to slump to the stone pavement, wet with his own blood. The Roman soldiers saw a great joke in this provincial Jew claiming to be a king. They threw a robe across His shoulders and placed a stick in His hand for a scepter. They still needed a crown to make their travesty complete. Small flexible branches covered with long thorns, commonly used for kindling fires in the charcoal braziers in the courtyard, were plaited into the shape of a crude crown. The crown was pressed into his scalp and again there was copious bleeding as the thorns pierced the very vascular tissue. After mocking Him and striking Him across the face, the soldiers took the stick from His hand and struck Him across the head, driving the thorns deeper into His scalp. Finally, they tired of their sadistic sport and tore the robe from His back. The robe had already become adherent to the clots of blood and serum in the wounds, and its removal, just as in the careless removal of a surgical bandage, caused excruciating pain. The wounds again began to bleed.

GOLGOTHA

In deference to Jewish custom, the Romans apparently returned His garments. The heavy patibulum of the cross was tied across His shoulders. The procession of the condemned Christ, two thieves, and the execution detail of Roman soldiers headed by a centurion began its slow journey along the route which we know today as the Via Dolorosa.

In spite of Jesus' efforts to walk erect, the weight of the heavy wooden beam, together with the shock produced by copious loss of blood, was too much. He stumbled and fell. The rough wood of the beam gouged into the lacerated skin and muscles of the shoulders. He tried to rise, but human muscles had been pushed beyond their endurance. The centurion, anxious to proceed with the crucifixion, selected a stalwart North African onlooker, Simon of Cyrene, to carry the cross. Jesus followed, still bleeding and sweating the cold, clammy sweat of shock. The 650-yard journey from the Fortress Antonia to Golgotha was finally completed. The prisoner was again stripped of His clothing except for a loin cloth which was allowed the Jews.

The crucifixion began. Jesus was offered wine mixed with myrrh, a mild analgesic, pain-reliving mixture. He refused the drink. Simon was ordered to place the patibulum on the ground, and Jesus was quickly thrown backward, with His shoulders against the wood. The legionnaire felt for the depression at the front of the wrist. He drove a heavy, square wrought-iron nail through the wrist and deep into the wood. Quickly, he moved to the other side and repeated the action, being careful not to pull the arms too tightly, but to allow some flexion and movement. The patibulum was then lifted into place at the top of the stipes, and the titulus reading "Jesus of Nazareth, King of the Jews" was nailed into place.

The left foot was pressed backward against the right foot. With both feet extended, toes down, a nail was driven through the arch of each, leaving the knees moderately flexed. The victim was now crucified.

ON THE CROSS

As Jesus slowly sagged down with more weight on the nails in the wrists, excruciating, fiery pain shot along the fingers and up the arms to explode in the brain. The nails in the wrists were putting pressure on the median nerve, large nerve trunks which traverse the mid-wrist and hand. As He pushed himself upward to avoid this stretching torment, He placed His full weight on the nail through His feet. Again there was searing agony as the nail tore through the nerves between the metatarsal bones of this feet.

At this point, another phenomenon occurred. As the arms fatigued, great waves of cramps swept over the muscles, knotting them in deep relentless, throbbing pain. With these cramps came the inability to push Himself upward. Hanging by the arm, the pectoral muscles, the large muscles of the chest, were paralyzed and the intercostal muscles, the small muscles between the ribs, were unable to *act. Air could be drawn into the lungs, but could not be exhaled. Jesus fought to raise Himself in order to get even one short breath. Finally, the carbon dioxide level increased in the lungs and in the blood stream, and the cramps partially subsided.*

THE LAST WORDS

Spasmodically, He was able to push Himself upward to exhale and bring in life-giving oxygen. It was undoubtedly during these periods that He uttered the seven short sentences that are recorded.

The first - looking down at the Roman soldiers throwing dice for His seamless garment: "Father, forgive them for they do not know what they do."

The second - to the penitent thief: "Today, thou shalt be with me in Paradise."

*The third - looking down at Mary **Jesus' mother,** He said: "Woman, behold your son."*
*Then turning to the terrified, grief-stricken adolescent John, the beloved apostle, He said: **"Behold your mother."***

The fourth cry is from the beginning of Psalm 22: "My God, My God, why have You forsaken Me?"

He suffered hours of limitless pain, cycles of twisting, joint-rending cramps, intermittent partial asphyxiation, and searing pain as tissue was torn from His lacerated back from His movement up and down against the rough timbers of the cross. Then another agony began: a deep crushing pain in the chest as the pericardium, the sac surrounding the heart, slowly filled with serum and began to compress the heart.
The prophecy in Psalm 22:14 was being fulfilled: "I am poured out like water, and all my bones are out of joint, my heart is like wax; it is melted in the midst of my bowels."

The end was rapidly approaching. The loss of tissue fluids had reached a critical level; the compressed heart was struggling to pump heavy, thick, sluggish blood to the tissues, and the tortured lungs were making a frantic effort to inhale small gulps of air. The markedly dehydrated tissues sent their flood of stimuli to the brain. Jesus gasped His fifth cry: "I thirst." Again we read in the prophetic psalm: "My strength is dried up like a potsherd; my tongue cleaveth to my jaws; and thou has brought me into the dust of death" (Psalm 22:15 KJV).

A sponge soaked in posca, the cheap, sour wine that was the staple drink of the Roman legionnaires, was lifted to Jesus' lips. His body was now in extremis, and He could feel the chill of death creeping through His tissues.

This realization brought forth His sixth word, possibly little more than a tortured whisper: "It is finished." His mission of atonement had been completed. Finally, He could allow His body to die. With one last surge of strength, He once again pressed His torn feet against the nail, straightened His legs, took a deeper breath, and uttered His seventh and last cry: "Father, into Your hands I commit My spirit."

DEATH

The common method of ending a crucifixion was by crurifracture, the breaking of the bones of the leg. This prevented the victim from pushing himself upward; the tension could not be relieved from the muscles of the chest, and rapid suffocation occurred. The legs of the two thieves were broken, but when the soldiers approached Jesus, they saw that this was unnecessary.

Apparently, to make doubly sure of death, the legionnaire drove his lance between the ribs, upward through the pericardium and into the heart. John 19:34 states, "And immediately there came out blood and water." Thus there was an escape of watery fluid from the sac surrounding the heart and the blood of the interior of the heart. This is rather conclusive post-mortem evidence that Jesus died, not the usual crucifixion death by suffocation, but of heart failure due to shock and constriction of the heart by fluid in the pericardium.

Read Matthew 27:26-66. What do you learn about Jesus as you think about what He went through? How does this make you feel about Him? How do you think He feels about doing this for you?

Write a prayer, sharing with Jesus how you feel about Him dying for your sins. Tell Him what you have learned about Him and how you feel about Him. Make this a real and personal letter from you to Him.

DAY 77
The Garden of Gethsemane

Jesus was and is so powerful that the grave could not hold Him. Jesus conquered death and after He was resurrected from the dead, he appeared to over 500 people (1 Corinthians 15:6).

Read John 20:1-13. What were the reactions of each of the people mentioned here? Why did the react the way they did? Which one could you relate to the most and why?

Reading John 20:14-18, why do you think Mary did not recognize Jesus when she saw Him? What is the significance of Mary recognizing Jesus when He said her name? What does Jesus tell us about God? Do you feel you have the relationship with God that Jesus is describing?

Read Luke 24:13-35. What did Jesus ask when they first saw Him? In verse 21, what were they hoping Jesus would do?

Focus on verses 25-27. What did Jesus tell them? How did He reveal God's plan regarding everything that had taken place?

Looking at verse 32, how did Jesus' company affect them? Have you ever had a time when the presence of the Lord affected you like that?

Read John 20:19-31. What happened the first time Jesus appeared? What did He tell them? How did Thomas react when he heard about what happened? What happened when Jesus appeared again? What did He tell Thomas? Do you think there are times that message is for you also? What was Thomas' reaction and what did Jesus say about it? What are we blessed with if we believe? Do you believe this is true?

Read John 21:1-25. Jesus appeared to them at the Sea of Tiberias, which is the Sea of Galilee. Why is the location significant? Who was there? What were they doing? What did Jesus ask them?

What did Peter do when he realized it was Jesus? Do you think Jesus loved his passion?

Why did Jesus ask them to bring some of the fish they caught to add to what He already had ready for them?

What did Jesus ask Peter? Why did He ask three times? What did Jesus tell Peter He wanted Him to do? What does this say about how Jesus will treat you if you ever have a time of failure? What does this tell you about how you should treat others who have failed you?

Read Matthew 28:16-20. Where were they when they meet with Jesus? What did Jesus tell them about Himself? What did He tell them to do? What did He promise them? What does Jesus want you to do? What does He promise you?

As you think about the 77 Days you have spent connecting with Jesus, what have you learned that you did not know before? When you think about Jesus, what stands out to you?

Write a prayer asking the Lord to show you who you are supposed to disciple. Make a commitment to go to them. Let Him know that you trust He will be with you when you do. Ask Him to bring to mind what He wants you to know about Him.

The goal of this journal was for you to get to know Jesus and to connect with Him in a meaningful way. Jesus lived a revolutionary life and He spawned a revolutionary movement that changed the world. I hope and pray that He changes your life in a radical way and that you are a part of seeing life change in other people.

May you know how much He loves you.
May you know the abundant life He has for you.
May you know that He is with you.
May you know Him!

▶ LIFE GROUP DISCUSSION QUESTIONS ◀

DISCUSS THESE QUESTIONS TOGETHER:

1. Read Matthew 21:12-17 and 1 Corinthians 6:19. What was Jesus' reaction when He entered the Temple? What does Jesus need to turn upside down, or clear out in you as the "Temple of God?"

2. Read Matthew 21:18-22. Imagine the kind of faith that could move mountains. What, if anything, is holding you back from having that kind of faith? Did you know that living out L.I.F.E, as we teach in our Growth Track Class, will teach you how to develop more faith?

3. The Kings of old, and even certain leaders today, are guilty of using people for their own achievements and successes. Some people even idolize those with such power and hope someday to be elevated to their status. Take time to read John 13:1-17 and discuss why what Jesus said is so contrary to the way many people perceive work, home life, and even church.

4. When you pray, do you ask God for exactly what you want in detail? Do you surrender the fulfillment of that prayer completely to God, however that answer may come? Or do you only see answered prayer as receiving exactly what you prayed for? After discussing, read: Matthew 26:36-46.

5. If someone told you that "all authority in Heaven and on earth had been given to them," what would you do with what they had to say? Would your first thought be, "Who does he think he is, and do I believe him?" Then if you did believe, would you do whatever he told you to do? Read Matthew 28:16-20.

▰LIFE GROUP DISCUSSION QUESTIONS◂

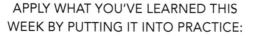

APPLY WHAT YOU'VE LEARNED THIS
WEEK BY PUTTING IT INTO PRACTICE:

LOVE LIKE JESUS

How do you know Jesus is the risen Christ? Read John 20:26-29. How can you begin to practice loving others the way Jesus loves us?

INTENTIONAL INTIMACY

What practices and habits could you start that will help you hear the voice of God?

FULLY SURRENDERED

What do you need to "surrender" in order to know the blessings of God?

EXPERIENCE MORE

Who needs to hear how you met Jesus and what it's meant to you, personally?

2/26/17

God will level my mountains

Yes to: good breaks, healing, new season
new strength, new doors open, unprecidented
favor

God will do things that will leave no doubt
That — it was the hand of God!

God wants to make me the example of his
blessings.

God will put an end to whats held me back

God said — Before you call — I will answer you!

Before I call — God will answer!

Quit living guilty — Trust that God knows where
I am — and I will know that it God coming
before me.